W9-ANJ-774

RENDEZVOUS WITH DESTINY:

The FDR Legacy

by

Amy Waters Yarsinske

THE
DONNING COMPANY
PUBLISHERS

The Donning Company Publishers
184 Business Park Drive, Suite 206
Virginia Beach, VA 23462

Steve Mull, General Manager
Barbara B. Buchanan, Office Manager
Jan Martin, Editorial Production Coordinator
Richard A. Horwege, Senior Editor
Marshall McClure, Graphic Designer
Julia Kilmer, Imaging Technician/Proofreader
Dennis Walton, Project Director
Anne Cordray, Project Research Coordinator
Scott Rule, Director of Marketing
Travis Gallup, Marketing Coordinator

Library of Congress Cataloging-in-Publication Data

Yarsinske, Amy Waters, 1963–
　　Rendezvous with destiny : the FDR legacy / by Amy Waters Yarsinske.
　　　p. cm.
　　Includes bibliographical references and index.
　　ISBN 1-57864-216-7 (soft cover : alk. paper)
　　　1. Roosevelt, Franklin D. (Franklin Delano), 1882–1945—
Influence. 2. Roosevelt, Franklin D. (Franklin Delano), 1882–1945—
Quotations. 3. United States—Politics and government—1933–1945. 4.
United States—Politics and government—1933–1945—Quotations,
maxims, etc. 5. New Deal, 1933–1939. 6. Roosevelt, Franklin D.
(Franklin Delano), 1882–1945—Pictorial works. 7. United States—
History—1933–1945—Pictorial works. 8. Franklin Delano Roosevelt
Memorial (Washington, D.C.) I. Title.

E807.Y37 2003
973.917'092—dc21
[B]   2003048901

Contents

4   **Introduction**

Chapter 1
10   **RENDEZVOUS WITH DESTINY**

Chapter 2
26   **A NEW DEAL FOR THE AMERICAN PEOPLE**

Chapter 3
38   **THE GREAT ARSENAL OF DEMOCRACY**

Chapter 4
56   **MOSES IN THE PROMISED LAND**

66   **Afterword   *THE FDR LEGACY***

74   **Endnotes**

75   **Bibliography**

77   **Index**

79   **About the Author**

80   **About the Contemporary Photography**

Introduction

The men who got Franklin Delano Roosevelt elected president of the United States consisted of five individuals—Frank C. Walker, W. Forbes Morgan, Bernard M. Baruch, and Henry Morgenthau—both father and son—who had the money and campaign savvy to put Roosevelt in the White House. They, in turn, gathered men around FDR who were the most active in planning to meet future problems.

They formed the "brain trust" and were picked primarily by Louis Howe and Judge Samuel I. Rosenman. "They were a group with whom Franklin consulted in laying plans to meet the problems that all of us were aware had to be met by whoever was elected president in 1932," wrote Eleanor Roosevelt shortly after her husband's death. "There were lawyers, professors, politicians, all gathered together to think out ways and means of doing specific things."[10] The original "brain trust" consisted of Professors Raymond A. Moley and Rexford G. Tugwell, and Judge Sam Rosenman. Later, writes Eleanor, Adolf A. Berle was brought in, and on certain occasions Dr. Joseph McGoldrick, Richard Gilbert and General Hugh Johnson were consulted. When Moley later became a critic of the New Deal, he was replaced on the team, but in the opinion of his colleagues—fellow "brain-trusters"—he'd been the clearest thinker of them all.

"Through the whole of Franklin's career there never was any deviation from his original objective—to help make life better for the average man, woman, and child. A thousand and one means were used, difficulties arose, changes took place, but this objective always was the motive for whatever had to be done," Eleanor continued. This included the manner in which FDR's speeches were crafted and delivered to the public. While there are many examples of FDR's oversight of his speech preparation—and speechwriters—his acceptance speech at Chicago in 1932 is as good as any. The time between his nomination and acceptance by the Democratic Party as its presidential candidate necessitated little need to rush to write an acceptance speech too far in advance but when FDR opted to fly to the convention, its preparation—or at least an outline of it—was an absolute necessity. "Mr. Raymond Moley has stated that he wrote that acceptance speech," penned Eleanor. "I feel sure he was never aware of some of the things that happened in connection with it."[11] As it became clear, there were two versions of the speech sharing some similarities. "The fact is that my husband wrote one speech himself. It was dictated to a stenographer in Chicago over the [long distance] telephone from Albany, Franklin, Miss [Marguerite] LeHand, Miss [Grace] Tully, and Judge Rosenman taking turns at dictating."[12] The speech, as it was thus dictated, together with ones that Moley and Tugwell wrote as an improvement on it, were brought to FDR by Louis Howe when he met FDR and Eleanor at the Chicago airport. As Howe started to hand both versions to FDR, Roosevelt said: "Oh, I've revised it and have a new draft in my pocket. I have been working on it on the plane."[13] The one in his pocket was, as it turned out, the speech delivered at the Chicago convention hall. "He'd read through the others," continued Eleanor, "and conceded to mention what Howe felt were important points and that were not in Franklin's own revised draft."

As FDR entered the White House, and facing serious social and economic crises across the nation, he employed the speech-writing skills of men who were earthy and connected to the people. American novelist John Steinbeck, famous for his down-to-earth portrayals of human strife in the Great Depression, including *Grapes of Wrath*, involved himself in political campaigns and issues. He made substantial contributions to Franklin Roosevelt's last campaign speeches, leading his critics to conclude he was a New Dealer with an agenda. But quite to the contrary Steinbeck held his own on every issue. Middlebury College instructor Jay Parini called Steinbeck a "New Deal Democrat with a fierce admixture of western individualism and Yankee independence," though there are those who point to Steinbeck's own words as proof of his leftist leanings: "There are as many communist systems as there are communists."[14] Nevertheless, his writing was so fluid and in touch with the public sentiment that Roosevelt overlooked Steinbeck's personal politics, capitalizing on the writer's ability to identify with and describe the American people. But

FDR also had a fondness for the ability of Archibald MacLeish, the lawyer, man of letters, and accomplished poet who became librarian of Congress in 1939. MacLeish wrote speeches for FDR, including most of the 1941 inaugural address, and gave regular radio broadcasts championing administration policies.

The president's in-house speechwriters grew accustomed to keeping lookout for the president from the windows of the Cabinet Room as he tooled up the covered walk in his armless wheelchair, his hands clutching documents he was reading, and in his mouth, a cigarette holder tilted at the usual jaunty angle. Fala ran alongside with the president's Secret Service detail not far behind. Sam Rosenman described the scene well, noting remarkably all the time he'd spent in that room writing the president's speeches. It was in the Cabinet Room that nearly all of Roosevelt's famous speeches and messages were assembled. The room's large table, air-conditioning, and seclusion from the hustle and bustle of daily West Wing business made it the perfect location for the president and his speechwriters. When a speech was in full bloom, the room was a shambles. The night of February 21, 1942, Rosenman observed was one of those nights when the Cabinet Room would've startled the most studied observer of their work.

When the president needed a speech, Rosenman and his team

went into action. As soon as Roosevelt finished dictating inserts, his speechwriters—led by Rosenman—quickly sized up the president's comments as far from any coherent form. They returned to the Cabinet Room and started drafting the actual speech. This could go on for days and nights tied together end to end. Most of Roosevelt's work on speeches was accomplished during the evening. Rosenman, Harry L. Hopkins, Robert E. Sherwood, and often others gathered for FDR's standard cocktail ceremony in the oval study at quarter past seven, the president behind his desk mixing drinks and carrying on a steady conversation.

Around midnight on February 21, lights burning, but a black curtain drawn over the windows as the country was at war, the top of the table in the Cabinet Room could hardly be found. "At one end of the table," wrote Rosenman, "was a large tray; on it were a big thermos

pitcher of coffee, two piles of sandwiches covered by a damp napkin, a large number of bottles of beer, Coca-Cola, ginger ale, and plain charged water, some cups and saucers and large glasses, a bowl of cracked ice, and a bottle of whisky."[15] Seated around the table were three men—the president's hard-working team of speechwriters— sleeves drawn up and dead tired as they'd been working all day on a speech. Having just said their goodnights to the president in his White House study, they walked over to the Cabinet Room to do more work on the speech, a tray of food and drinks awaited them at the direction of the president. Sherwood, Rosenman recalled later, poured himself a whisky and soda; Harry Hopkins helped himself to a cup of black coffee and a sandwich; and Rosenman helped himself to a Coke and two sandwiches. "I phoned upstairs to the four stenographers who had been asked to report for duty at 11:00 p.m. to work with us," he continued, to let them know there were sandwiches and beverages for them in the Cabinet Room also.

Roosevelt expected the draft the next morning with his breakfast. Grace Tully, in her office, typed inserts and corrections that the president dictated during their last session of the evening in his study. After a new draft was finished, she'd come in and quietly hand a fresh copy to each of them, take the new pieces of the speech and retreat to her office to start the corrected draft process all over again. "As we drank, we huddled over the new inserts she had brought in," recalled Rosenman, "We were working on a fireside chat the president was to deliver on Washington's Birthday, 1942."[16]

"'Let's see now,' Rosenman said, 'this is draft six'"—so he took a carbon copy of draft five, which the president had last seen in his study. He changed the five to a six, keeping the original draft on which the president had made deletions and corrections in his own hand. "'He certainly has the geography and strategy of the war at his finger tips,'" observed Rosenman, as he reread some of the pages. "'He makes it sound as simple and understandable as he did the banking crisis back in 1933. It was damned smart of him to ask the people to spread out their maps of the world and follow him when he speaks—that's the way they'll get it and understand what the strategy is all about.'"[17] The speech was important. The Washington's Birthday speech was FDR's first fireside chat since December 9, 1941, two days after the Japanese attack on Pearl Harbor. In early 1942, American forces were being beaten back badly, and the public seemed to be barraged with bad news. Rosenman had included a passage in the speech that the president had cut. "'I think he thought it was too optimistic and promised too much good news too soon,'" said Hopkins, as he poured himself another highball. "'One thing the president does not want to do is to kid the American people into believing that this is anything but a tough son-of-a-bitch of a war against the toughest and cruelest bastards on earth.'"[18] But the team was also able to convince the president to drop two pages of dictated comments from the day before, so tradeoffs were a constant part of massaging a speech to its final draft. Work on the Washington's Birthday speech continued through the night as Rosenman's team polished, corrected, added and deleted text for the president's perusal over breakfast. When it was done, Hopkins and Sherwood retreated to the Willard Hotel, where they shared a small apartment. They'd not smelled fresh air since breakfast the day before.

Nearly every major speech FDR delivered was a policy-making speech, and as Rosenman duly noted, "those who are around when it is being prepared and while it is going through its many drafts, with numerous changes and insertions and deletions, are in a peculiarly strategic position to help shape that policy."[19] Rosenman himself coined the phrase *New Deal*, which brought together Roosevelt's myriad of economic and social reconstruction programs under one banner. Rosenman and his team also understood the limit of their influence. When FDR was available again after one of the team's all-nighters, he'd look immediately at the last page of the draft for its number whereupon he announced that at least 92 percent of it must be cut. He then began to read through the draft, pausing along the way to dictate "Insert A" or "Insert G" and so on. Each time he decided to dictate something he said, he'd bellow, "'Grace, take a law,' a line he gladly borrowed from the Kaufman-Hart-Rodgers musical *I'd Rather Be Right* in which George M. Cohan plays the part of FDR."[20] But the team, largely among Roosevelt's closest advisors on matters of economics and social policy, were not yes men—they often argued their point and FDR argued his. Rosenman, Hopkins and Sherwood learned the best time to spar with him, often retreating on an earlier draft only to come back with greater success on draft six or seven. In some drafts of a speech, paragraphs show up in one draft and reappear in another. "This means," said Rosenman, "that the speech-writing team reinserted something that the president had taken out, and tried again to persuade him to keep it in. Sometimes we succeeded," he continued, "sometimes we failed."[21]

Many have asked through the years since Roosevelt's passing why the president didn't craft his own speeches when they were so critical to the development of policy during his successive presidencies. Why did he need aides to write them for him? "Basically, the answer is this," wrote Rosenman in *Working with Roosevelt*, "The speeches as finally delivered were his—and his alone—no matter who the collaborators were. He had gone over every point, every word, time and again. He had studied, reviewed, and read aloud each draft, and had changed it again and again, either in his own handwriting, by dictating inserts, or making deletions. Because of the many hours he spent in its preparation, by the time he delivered a speech he knew it almost by heart." No, FDR did not sit down and write his speeches from start to finish—with there being one or two exceptions. Presidential scholars argue that Roosevelt ascribed speeches to himself that he did not write—and this is true—even going so far as to put up a big front that he wrote every word. But arguably, Rosenman points to the president's lack of time in the day to prepare a speech. Some of FDR's speeches or messages took as many as ten days to prepare, and very few took less than three. Though this was not actual writing time, it did include review of reports, memoranda, proposed drafts, information, and statistics. The president's schedule would never have permitted him the time to complete the preliminaries and draft preparation necessary to carry a speech from start to finish. The president often asked Rosenman to produce a full draft or certain paragraphs in it to be checked by several departments or agencies. During World War II, Robert Sherwood went so far as to clear the president's speeches through the head of British intelligence in the United States, William S. Stephenson, better known by his New York cable address: Intrepid,[22] before they were delivered. Sherwood, though Roosevelt's trusted speechwriter, was later an Office of Strategic Services (OSS) agent, precursor to the Central Intelligence Agency (CIA), as well as a well-known playwright.

While many men prepared his speeches, the speeches were his own from the delivery perspective. During press conferences and fireside chats, his own speaking style, his use of stories and jokes, he used because he wanted people to know him. Friend and journalist Frank Kingdon once took Roosevelt a paper he'd prepared at the president's request setting forth an idea he was thinking of including in a fireside chat. The president read it quickly, according to Kingdon, then went over it sentence by sentence, changing a word here, transposing sentences there. But he came to one sentence, paused, looked at Kingdon square in the eye and said, "You thought that was pretty good when you wrote it, didn't you?" Kingdon smiled and answered, "Yes, sir. I thought that was about the best sentence in the paper." With a dramatic flourish, Roosevelt picked up a blue pencil and ran a heavy line through it. They both laughed. He didn't want any fancy rhetoric in one of his speeches—it wasn't his style. FDR endeared himself to the public, becoming the people's confidante by constantly calling them "My friends. . . ." His fireside chats were prepared speeches, such as the Washington Birthday speech on which Rosenman and his colleagues labored long, but their message was always clear. The sentence that is key to all the fireside chats made during FDR's presidency was in the one he delivered on April 14, 1938, in which he says, "I never forget that I live in a house owned by all the American people and that I have been given their trust." And the tone of all of them is illustrated best by a paragraph from a fireside chat delivered in 1934:

A few timid people who fear progress will try to give you new and strange names for what we are doing. Sometimes they will call it "fascism," sometimes "communism," sometimes "regimentation," sometimes "socialism." But, in so doing, they are trying to make very complex and theoretical something that is really very simple and very practical. I believe in practical explanations and in practical politics. I believe that what we are doing today is a necessary fulfillment of old and tested American ideals.

Decades after his death, subsequent generations of Americans want to know the source of this president's intimate contact with those he called "My friends. . . ." How was he able to cement a relationship with so many millions of people in all corners of the world, of a wide array of races, religions, and creeds. There was much more to it than a moving radio voice, Rosenman observed. "I think that the great reason for Roosevelt's place in the hearts and heads of people was his ability to make them feel that he associated himself personally with each of them in each one's aspirations for something better in life. He did not seem to be someone far removed, fighting their battles in a rarefied atmosphere. He was," in Rosenman's opinion, "right down in the sweaty arena with them, side by side, expressing what they were thinking, doing what they wanted done, taking his strength and his boldness from their strength and their support."[23] The bottom line is that Roosevelt's magic touch with the American memory comes down to his personality. He thought in terms of human beings rather than abstract, unattainable objectives. One newspaper that had largely opposed the president during his four terms wrote at the time of his death, "Men will thank God on their knees, a hundred years from now, for Roosevelt's leadership."[24] Add to that the comment of a close friend, who often argued vigorously with FDR, "Now we are on our own."[25]

I HAVE SEEN WAR

I HAVE SEEN WAR ON LAND AND SEA
BLOOD RUNNING FROM THE WOUND
SEEN THE DEAD IN THE MUD. I HAVE
DESTROYED... I HAVE SEEN CHILDREN
I HAVE SEEN THE AGONY OF MOTHE

I HATE WAR

Governor Franklin D. Roosevelt, on the campaign trail in 1932, delivered many speeches that brought a fresh personality, new ideas and hope to the American people. Each of his campaign speeches foreshadowed his future New Deal programs. Passing through Detroit, Michigan, on October 2, Roosevelt said, "In these days of difficulty, we Americans everywhere must and shall choose the path of social justice, the path of faith, the path of hope and the path of love toward our fellow men." His closest advisers described his stumping across America as more a "triumphant tour" than campaigning for office. (FDR Presidential Library.)

"His life must . . . be regarded as one of the commanding events in human destiny,"[26] wrote British Prime Minister Winston Churchill shortly after FDR's death in April 1945. While the president certainly lived his life fully in the present, he realized both his strong connections to the past and the important events of each day that seemed to push him ever closer to his rendezvous with destiny. Controlling his own life's ambitions fed his role as commander-in-chief not only of his own country, but also in many respects, as Churchill notes, "events in human destiny."

By the time he concluded his 1932 campaign trips through the heartland of America, Franklin Roosevelt felt the Depression could be beaten. "From him," wrote Eleanor, "I learned how to observe from train windows: He would watch the crops, notice how people dressed, how many cars there were and in what condition, and even look at the wash on the clothes lines. When the CCC [Civilian Conservation Corps] was set up, he knew, though he never made a note, exactly where work of various kinds was needed. Franklin saw geography clearly."[27] FDR felt most of what he observed, despite shortcomings and wastefulness, demonstrated most strongly the vitality of the people and their ability to pull themselves out of the depths of hard economic times. Eleanor Roosevelt believed it was from his faith in the people that he drew the words of his first inaugural address: "The only thing we have to fear is fear itself."

The campaign speeches, and later the fireside chats, as they came to be popularly known, entailed a great deal of work on FDR's part. During his first campaign—and the three to follow—the subjects were carefully chosen, the places and times to speak discussed with his "brain trust," and the research begun. "Franklin expected the people assigned to this to bring him arguments on both sides of the question and as much information on the subject as it was possible to gather," observed Eleanor. "He went over all their material carefully and picked out the facts that were to go into the speech; then he gave it, after considerable discussion, to those whom he entrusted with the writing of the first draft."[28] FDR's speechwriters would bring the draft back, he'd take a look at it again, and back and forth they'd go with subsequent drafts. If he didn't like what he was seeing put in front of him, the president occasionally called in many different people for advice and assistance. "I have known him," Eleanor continued, "even after a draft had been submitted for literary criticism to the best person . . . to read the final copy over and over again, put in words or take them out, transpose sentences and polish it until he knew it by heart and it completely represented his own thought."

The process of writing a speech for FDR was made more difficult by Eleanor's account of his need to make the words his own. Judge Sam Rosenman was particularly skilled at getting a Roosevelt speech from draft to delivery, coaxing the president through the words and agreeing to some-times-minor modifications to make FDR more comfortable with the final product. "The essentials in an important speech," wrote Eleanor, "must remain, because it is necessary to get in everything that will clarify the subject; yet it must not be complicated by the addition of even one unnecessary word. As many as ten people might work on a speech, but in the last stages, two or three would do the paring."[29] If they persisted in not getting it right, FDR went to what he called his speech-material file, kept by Marguerite A. LeHand, who had been his personal secretary for eighteen years and who quickly became the same when he ascended to the presidency. This file contained anything that had caught Roosevelt's eye, either in the mail or in the press or in the course of reading articles, memoranda or books that he felt pertained to a speech he had to deliver.

xxxxxxxxxxxxxxxxxxxxxxxxxxxxx

AGRICULTURE

★

What Is Wrong
and
What To Do About It

★

Governor
Franklin D. Roosevelt's
Speech
at Topeka, Kansas
September 14,
1932

Issued by
THE DEMOCRATIC NATIONAL COMMITTEE
Hotel Biltmore, New York City

xxxxxxxxxxxxxxxxxxxxxxxxxxxxx

Roosevelt spelled out his strategy for farm relief in his September 14, 1932, speech at Topeka, Kansas. The Democratic National Committee turned the speech into a brochure and distributed it widely throughout the country. As governor of New York, Roosevelt developed a comprehensive program of farm relief, winning over traditionally Republican farmers in his own state. When he spoke of sweeping changes to America's farming industry, farmers listened: He was proposing, after all, tax strategies, government responsibility—his own promise to farmers to help them along. (Author's collection.)

No citizen who heard or read the speeches Governor Roosevelt made on the campaign trail had any reason to be surprised at any part of Roosevelt's New Deal program. The one exception was his Pittsburgh speech made on October 19, 1932. Roosevelt would reflect later that this speech—in the heat of the campaign—was delivered without enough time for adequate discussion and deliberation. He spoke of reducing government spending, and while a cut in expenditures was an obvious pledge of the Democratic platform that year, Roosevelt's New Deal package was going to cost large sums of money. Had he thought it through, Roosevelt would not have gone out on such a long, unsupportable limb in Pittsburgh. Four years later, just before the start of the 1936 reelection campaign, President Roosevelt told Judge Samuel I. Rosenman, the president's longtime friend, adviser, and speechwriter, that he wanted to make his first major campaign speech in Pittsburgh to explain his 1932 statement on expenditures. Rosenman quipped: "Mr. President, the only thing you can say about that 1932 speech is to deny categorically that you ever made it."[1] Both men laughed. Roosevelt went on to carry forty-two states, handily winning the White House. (FDR Presidential Library.)

"In preparing a speech," wrote the president, "I usually take the various drafts and suggestions which have been submitted to me and also the material which has been accumulated in the speech file on various subjects, read them carefully, lay them aside, and then dictate my own draft, usually to Miss [Grace] Tully [his stenographer]. Naturally," he continued, "the final speech will contain some of the thoughts and even some of the sentences, which appeared in some of the drafts or suggestions submitted."[30] Arguably, however, his speechwriters usually contributed more to the speeches than he credits—and vice versa. In the decades since FDR's death, his "brain trust" and some of the on again/off again cadre of his speechwriters claim provenance over Roosevelt's presidential speeches, particularly the famous ones. The president remarked in his own writings that he supposed it is human that two or three of the many persons with whom he had consulted in the preparation of speeches should seek to give the impression that they have been responsible for the writing of the speeches, and that one or two of them should claim authorship or should state that some other individual was the author. Such assertions, he bluntly retorted, are not accurate. "On some of my speeches," FDR continued, "I have prepared as many as five or six successive drafts myself after reading drafts and suggestions submitted by other people and I have changed drafts from time to time after consulting with other people either personally or by telephone."[31] But there are those

This generation of Americans has a rendezvous with destiny. . . .

Acceptance speech to the Democratic National Convention for renomination as presidential candidate for a second term, Philadelphia, Pennsylvania, June 27, 1936.

who contend that Roosevelt's inaugural speeches, in particular, demonstrate the advantages of full-scale ghostwriting, although the president encouraged the myth that he wrote his famous first inaugural address in one vigorous night's work at Hyde Park.[32] According to biographer Kenneth Davis, FDR hand-copied a draft by speechwriter Raymond Moley, apparently so it would look like his own work. This soon became a pattern that repeated itself often, regardless of the impression given by the president and first lady. Roosevelt's speeches maintained consistency, cadence, and clever wordplay because gifted aides, also his speechwriters, had crafted them. A few of the president's speechwriters, both before and after FDR's death, avoided attribution of his speeches to their wit and wisdom, deferring to the president as the author. Raymond Moley and Samuel Beer later came out and said which of Roosevelt's speeches they crafted. Others would do the same.

President Franklin D. Roosevelt rode in an open car after his inauguration with Eleanor (center) and Arkansas Democratic Senator Joseph T. Robinson, who was also Senate majority leader from 1933 until his death on July 14, 1937, in Washington, D.C. (FDR Presidential Library.)

FDR had moments, too, when a speech was in its final stages and when handed a copy, tore it up and dictated it from the beginning because he felt his speechwriters had not made it clear enough for the layman to understand. "Franklin had a gift for simplification. He often insisted," wrote the former first lady, "on putting in simple stories, drawn from conversations with visitors or friends in Warm Springs or Hyde Park, where his opportunity was greatest for close contact with people who talked to him as a human being and not as a public official. These illustrations, I think, helped him to give many people the feeling that he was talking to them in their own living rooms, and that they

"THE ONLY THING WE HAVE TO FEAR IS FEAR ITSELF--"

1933

MARCH 4, 1933

Inaugurated to his first term in office on March 4, 1933, President Franklin D. Roosevelt proclaimed: "The only thing we have to fear is fear itself." (FDR Presidential Library.)

knew and understood the complicated problems of government."[33] When asked on occasion if she'd had any role in the crafting of her husband's speeches, Eleanor Roosevelt often equivocated that while it was true FDR sometimes used parts of letters or paragraphs from articles she gave him to look at, and that she often read his speeches before he actually delivered them, she played no role at all. She was the first to tell him if she liked his delivery of a speech, and if for any reason she disapproved of it, said nothing.

Charles Michelson, then director of publicity for the Democratic National Committee (DNC), observed that even as governor of New York and presidential candidate of his party, Roosevelt often confounded his speechwriting team. Governor Roosevelt was scheduled to deliver a campaign speech at Oglethorpe University in Atlanta, Georgia, on April 22, 1932. Looking at Rosenman's prepared remarks, the governor asked questions and set into motion further work on the speech. The Oglethorpe speech turned out to be a key address. A small group of New York newspapermen that included Walter Brown of the Associated Press, James Kieran of *The New York Times*, Louis Ruppel of the *New York Daily News*, and Ernest K. Lindley of *Newsweek* came down to Roosevelt's retreat in Warm Springs, for a picnic with the governor. Everyone was having a good time, according to Rosenman. After a while the newspapermen began ribbing Roosevelt about some of his more recent speeches. He replied, in good fun, "Well, if you boys don't like my speeches, why don't you take a hand at drafting one yourselves." Lindley piped up, "I will," and he did, much to Rosenman's surprise. His colleagues did some brainstorming and editing with Lindley, but the final product was Lindley's draft. Roosevelt made a few changes, leaving the theme of the speech alone, "the country needs . . . the country demands bold, persistent experimentation." The latter phrase subsequently became watchwords for the New Deal.[34] The speech also forecast another important part of Roosevelt's program for recovery and economic stability: purchasing power for consumers rather than accumulation of capital for the producer.[35]

A few months later in the campaign, Michelson, Hugh Johnson and Raymond Moley were called to the governor's mansion to draft a speech to be delivered on August 30, 1932, in Columbus, Ohio. "Each of us had his manuscript with him," Michelson recalled. "They were three great speeches: resounding, earnest, and affirmative."[36] He noted that

Johnson's speech bristled with fulmination against the enemy and was peppered with wisecracks over the incompetence of the Hoover administration. Moley presented economic and social issues, and as a recognized economist, really knew his material. Michelson's contribution was pure politics, with some covert digs and clever insinuations of which Michelson observed he was especially proud. Unfortunately, from the speechwriters' perspective, none of these speeches was delivered. Governor Roosevelt dismissed his writing team back to their typewriters and yet another discussion ensued over content. Then, in a move that would subsequently become well known among his speechwriters, Roosevelt reclined on a couch and dictated his own version, occasionally, according to Michelson, using one of their phrases but generally culling the best ideas that had been submitted and putting them in his own words. "So far as I know," wrote a bemused Michelson, "this was the practice with every speech. Moley, Johnson, Stanley High, Tom Corcoran, and Judge Rosenman may sometime have fared better, but I was never present when a big speech was born that the president didn't take the political viands offered and cook them in his individual way. Take it from me, I'm rather experienced in the formation and presentation of speeches: Franklin Roosevelt is a better phrasemaker than anybody he ever had around him."[37]

The president's first inaugural address bore Roosevelt's distinctive style, the same style that had marked his informal addresses—fireside

Eleanor Roosevelt called the inauguration of her husband on March 4, 1933, "very, very solemn and a little terrifying," disturbing to her "because when Franklin got to that part of his speech when he said it might become necessary for him to assume powers ordinarily granted to a president in war time, he received the biggest ovation."[2] A despairing nation was anointing its new president with broad powers— and as Eleanor further observed, "One has a feeling of going it blindly because we're in a tremendous stream, and none of us knows where we're going to land." President Roosevelt (seated in the car), Eleanor, and others are pictured here in nation's capital in the summer of 1933. (FDR Presidential Library.)

In his first term, President Roosevelt immersed himself in carrying out a quick succession of messages to the Congress asking for legislation need to carry out his pledges of a New Deal. By September 30, 1934, when this photograph was taken of the president before a fireside chat, opposition had begun to mount against his reforms. In his speeches and messages in 1934, Roosevelt began to express himself forcibly against opponents of the New Deal. The premise of his September 30 fireside chat was simple: "We are moving forward to greater freedom, to greater security for the average man." (FDR Presidential Library.)

> ## I pledge you, I pledge myself, to a New Deal for the American people.
>
> *FDR's acceptance remarks for his party's nomination as presidential candidate, delivered at the Democratic National Convention, Chicago, Illinois, July 2, 1932.*

chats—that he began as governor of New York. Delivered on March 4, 1933, the purpose of the speech was twofold. "I sought principally ... to banish, so far as possible, the fear of the present and of the future which held the American people and the American spirit in its gasp . . . I promised a program of action: first to put people to work; and second, to correct the abuses . . . which had in great measure contributed to the crisis,"[38] said the president shortly afterwards. The first inaugural address was, in Rosenman's opinion, one of Roosevelt's great speeches, not only in its form and substance but also in accomplishment. It contained one of the immortal statements that has since come to personify Roosevelt: "The only thing we have to fear is fear itself. . . ." The speech itself was short, but it contained all the key elements of his program. The speech was also one of the very few the president wrote the first draft in his own hand. Using yellow legal cap paper, and sitting by a roaring fire at Hyde Park on the night of February 27, 1933, "I started it about 9:00 p.m. and ended at 1:30 a.m. A number of minor changes were made in subsequent drafts but the final draft is substantially the same as this original," wrote Roosevelt. But the president's original longhand draft does not include the famous "fear" sentence, observed Rosenman. From his longhand version a typewritten copy was made. After arriving in Washington, however, he revised the typewritten copy in his suite at the Mayflower Hotel. The final draft was typed the day before the speech was delivered, and it is in this last draft that the president adds the "fear" sentence.[39]

Franklin D. Roosevelt (second from right) was joined aboard the yacht Sewana *by this sons (left to right) John, Franklin Jr., and James, on July 14, 1936. The yacht master seated in the foreground is unidentified. (FDR Presidential Library.)*

Within the first one hundred days of his first term in office, President Franklin D. Roosevelt started many programs intended to help Americans pull themselves out of the Great Depression—popularly dubbed the New Deal. Created by the National Industrial Recovery Act on June 16, 1933, the Public Works Administration (PWA) budgeted several billion dollars to be spent on the construction of public works as a means of providing employment, stabilizing purchasing power, improving public welfare, and contributing to a revival of American industry. Simply put, it was designed to spend "big bucks on big projects." One of these projects was New York's Tri-Borough Bridge, which reaped the benefit of public works money made available through the PWA. "Like a modern flying carpet, the Tri-Borough Bridge swings across the sky with 'Baghdad on the Subway' in the background," noted the caption on this Roosevelt administration photograph, taken shortly after the bridge's completion in July 1936. In actuality, the Tri-Borough Bridge, New York's "flying carpet," was constructed as the centerpiece of a seventeen-mile network of bridges and roads connecting Manhattan, Queens, and the Bronx. The new bridge, the progeny of Robert Moses, appointed in 1934 as the first head of the Tri-Borough Bridge Authority, provided a new approach to automobile circulation that relied on cloverleafs and long stretches of highway to move traffic efficiently to the city's vast grid of streets. (FDR Presidential Library.)

While waiting at the Capitol to go out onto the steps to deliver his address, he wrote in longhand on his reading copy a new sentence, an impulsive yet intuitive demonstration of his emotion as he stood patiently on the precipice of his destiny. "This is a day of consecration," he added. He ad-libbed the word *national* before *consecration* as he spoke the line. Rosenman is not sure exactly how the "fear" sentence came about, nor what might have sparked Roosevelt to include it. He also never asked him. As a statement, the "fear" sentence bears a striking resemblance to a statement about fear written by Henry David Thoreau: "Nothing is so much to be feared as fear."[40] Eleanor Roosevelt later told Rosenman that one of her friends provided the president a copy of some of Thoreau's writings just before the day of inauguration, and that the material was in the president-elect's suite at the hotel while this speech was being polished. It is Rosenman's feeling that Roosevelt read the phrase and it stuck in his mind, subsequently finding its way into the speech.

After his first election to the presidency, Roosevelt asked Rosenman what to do about the original "brain trust." Rosenman wanted it left intact as a staff to gather materials for study and for speeches, as a group with whom the president could speak candidly. The judge resisted the notion that members of the "brain trust" should be given administrative jobs in the new administration. The president disagreed. Raymond Moley was named assistant secretary of state; Tugwell became assistant secretary of agriculture; Berle did some work for a short time with the Reconstruction Finance Corporation; and Rosenman remained on the New York Supreme Court bench until October 1943, when the president asked him to

resign and devote himself completely to White House war efforts. Rosenman felt the president made an error in breaking up the original "brain trust," and ultimately the paths of those Roosevelt put in administrative roles parted from his own. The only function performed by the original "brain trust" after 1933 was helping with the president's speeches—but never as the team they once were. Gradually, months after FDR's election, the term *brain trust* applied not only to the original group but to many new faces who came to the nation's capital. They included Harry Hopkins, Tom Corcoran, Dean Acheson, Ben Cohen, William Woodin, William C. Bullitt, Joseph P. Kennedy, Felix Frankfurter (before his appointment to the U.S. Supreme Court), and many others.[41] During the first term, Rosenman's visits to Washington were almost always social ones. Outside a couple of calls for help on a speech, Rosenman had nothing to do with any of the speeches or messages of Roosevelt's first term until his acceptance speech of 1936. As long as Moley was in the capital, particularly in 1933, he supervised the president's speech preparation; Robert Sherwood also remained a key figure in this process. Most of the new names in the "brain trust" worked the speeches the bulk of the president's first term.

In 1934 and 1936, drought and dust storms ravaged America's Great Plains and added to the New Deal's relief burden. The Plains became "the Dust Bowl," with storms so severe, if enough particles were ingested, some people died, choking on the earth that had once born fruitful crops. But it was, ironically, small farmers' excessive cultivation and exploitation of the land that made it barren, their access to the land made possible by the overly permissive property rights structure of the Homestead Act of 1862. The man in this 1934 photograph braces himself against the debris and high winds of a dust storm. (FDR Presidential Library.)

Among American citizens there should be no forgotten men and no forgotten races.

Address at the dedication of the new chemistry building, Howard University, Washington, D.C., October 26, 1936.

This April 1935 Kodak view of a dust storm in Baca County, Colorado, demonstrates the enormity of the dust clouds that rolled through the Great Plains states during the peak of the Depression. The Easter Sunday storm shown here travels down a road and through the countryside. The frequency of these storms forced homesteaders off their land. (FDR Presidential Library.)

Judge Rosenman was continually struck by the thoroughness with which the issues were covered in Roosevelt's speeches. The president's campaign speech delivered in Cleveland on October 16, 1936, took night and day to prepare, but was completed more quickly, even for a campaign speech, which tends to be what speechwriters consider a creature of the moment. The theme of his second presidential campaign was founded on his rescue of industry, farming, labor and banking from complete collapse. Roosevelt could not afford to spend much personal time on these speeches both because of the work of the presidency and the whistle-stop pace of his campaign appearances. The important speeches often required in excess of a week to produce, with a considerable measure of planning before the intensive writing began. "I don't know what was the record number of distinct drafts of a single speech," speechwriter Robert E. Sherwood wrote later, "but it must have been well over twelve, and in the final draft there might not be one sentence that survived from the first draft."[42] There were, of course, numerous routine speeches of a ceremonial nature that Sherwood observed were not considered of major significance but, in wartime, even in these Roosevelt was aware that he had a world audience and that everything he said might be material for the propaganda which flooded the airwaves.

Franklin Roosevelt's voice lent itself remarkably to the radio, and he was often on the airwaves—the first president to truly reap its benefit—to give speeches and fireside chats. It was a natural gift, Eleanor noted of his voice, for in his whole life he never had a lesson in diction or public speaking. "His voice unquestionably helped him to make the people of the country feel that they were an intelligent and understanding part of every government undertaking during his administration."[43] Roosevelt's voice and his ability to connect with the public delivering

Barefoot and sitting on fence like birds on a clothesline, the children in this Depression-era picture, their mother standing in the background, were the people of the American Plains the president wanted most to help—and they are the generation that largely revered Roosevelt, the only president many knew in their youth. (Author's collection.)

The Works Progress Administration (WPA) provided funding to New York–born artist Conrad A. Albrizio (1894–1973) to paint his murals in New York, Detroit, Alabama, and Louisiana. "The New Deal," Albrizio's tribute to President Roosevelt, was placed in the auditorium of the Leonardo Da Vinci Art School at 149 East Thirty-fourth Street in New York City in 1934. (FDR Presidential Library.)

Men and nature must work hand in hand. The throwing out of balance of the resources of nature throws out of balance also the lives of men.

Message to Congress on the use of our natural resources, Washington, D.C., January 24, 1935.

speeches led his advisors to craft speeches specifically intended for radio. But like every Roosevelt speech for some important purpose, whether it was a special occasion or not, the president discussed it first at some length with his close friends and advisors Harry Hopkins and Sam Rosenman, as well as speechwriter Robert Sherwood, communicating to each man what particular point he wanted to make, what sort of audience he wished to reach, and what the maximum word count was to be. Roosevelt generally low-balled his word count, setting impossibly few words as his parameter for a speech. Sherwood later remembered that he dictated pages and pages, approaching his main topic, sometimes hitting it squarely on the nose with terrific impact, sometimes rambling so far away from it that he couldn't get back to the main thrust of the speech. When the latter happened, Roosevelt's usual comment was, "Well—something along those lines—you and the boys can fix it up."[44] The "boys" often had to get to work out of necessity or the president wouldn't have had a speech to deliver—period. "I think he greatly enjoyed the sessions," Sherwood postulated later, especially, "when he felt free to say anything he pleased, uttering all kinds of personal insults, with the knowledge that none of it need appear in the final version."[45]

Roosevelt's vibrato before the public hardly resonated within the confines of the White House, where he rarely shared his most personal thoughts. FDR was born to a father over the age of 50 who, had he lived, would've been 104 years of age had he seen his son inaugurated president. Though his father was gone, Roosevelt remembered his birthdays, and that his father was born during the administration of John Quincy Adams. One day he turned to Grace Tully as he dated a document and said, "This is the anniversary of my father's birth." "Really, Mr. President," she responded. "How old would he be?" "He would have been 112 today," the president answered. This was after he'd been elected to his third term.[46]

Nothing was more private to the president than his polio. Columnist and political commentator Frank Kingdon first met the president in September 1936. They quickly became close friends, even though the subject of Kingdon's first chat with FDR had to

President Roosevelt breaks for lunch at the Grand Coulee Dam, ninety miles west of Spokane in the Columbia Basin, Washington, on October 2, 1937. The president had authorized $60 million for its construction in 1933. The Grand Coulee Dam was intended to create, in the broader scheme of the New Deal, a milk-and-honey Promised Land for Americans displaced by the Dust Bowl—the heartland of America ravaged by drought. The planned project included small farms of about eighty acres that the Roosevelt administration hoped would be occupied by families from the Midwest who had lost their land at the peak of the Great Depression. In his fireside chat ten days later, on October 12, the president spoke of the Grand Coulee Dam. "The engineer in charge told me that almost half of the whole cost of that dam to date had been spent for materials that were manufactured east of the Mississippi River, giving employment and wages to thousands of industrial workers in the eastern third of the Nation, two thousand miles away," Roosevelt told the American people. "All this world needs, of course, is a more business-like system of planning, [and] a greater foresight than we use today." FDR called for the creation of seven planning regions in which local people could originate and coordinate recommendations as to the kind of work to take place in each region of the country. (FDR Presidential Library.)

do with his disability. Surprisingly, Roosevelt spoke openly to Kingdon, "My Missus mentioned it the other day. You know, I can't get around as much as I'd like to, so she goes a lot of places I'd like to go." Eleanor's travels were invaluable to her husband because so many people wouldn't give him their honest assessment as president, but they spoke frankly with her. Eleanor went across the country and eventually to far-flung war zones to praise the troops for their commander-in-chief. FDR accepted his limitation, but he didn't

advertise it. While his disability deepened his appreciation of the human condition, it also toughened him. He did not permit photographs of himself in his wheelchair and today there are only three known pictures of him sitting in it held by public collections and possibly others in private ones—pictures that are respectfully protected by their owners.

FDR rationalized and worked around his handicap. Kingdon observed his patience, to which the president quipped, "If you had spent two years trying to get a slight movement in your toe, and then tasted the triumph of having it actually move, you too would learn something about patience."[47] Roosevelt carried his disability with dignity. But when he wanted to bring his son James into the White House as his secretary, his uncle, Frederic Delano, told him it would only draw criticism. Disappointed and feeling chastised, he retorted, "You know, Uncle Delano, I've got to have somebody I can trust to be my legs."[48] According to Kingdon, FDR once told Wendell Willkie something similar when Willkie wanted to know why Harry Hopkins was around so much. The media deserved much of the credit for the decency with which they treated the president's physical disability. He only spoke of it twice in public: the first time during his campaign for the New York governorship, and only because his opponents made it an issue; the other was after his return from the Yalta Conference in February 1945. Before making a speech before Congress, he asked to deliver his speech seated since it was easier for him than trying to stand with ten pounds of steel braces around his legs. In truth, he was in failing health and wanted no one to know it.

Because of his disability, Eleanor, whom he called "the Missus" or "my Missus," was her husband's best scout. He had in Eleanor a good reporter who knew how to look for what he would have seen if he had been with her, remarked Kingdon after the president's death. He relied on her reports, and would often check somebody else's with the comment, "That doesn't jibe with what the Missus said."[49] While FDR often asked Eleanor to travel on his behalf, she also chose often to go off on her own. One morning she left the White House to visit a prison in Baltimore but it was so early she chose not to wake the president. When FDR came down for breakfast, he called Eleanor's secretary, Malvina

> **In these days of difficulty, we Americans everywhere must and shall choose the path of social justice, the path of faith, the path of hope and the path of love toward our fellow men.**
>
> *Campaign address, Detroit, Michigan, October 2, 1932.*

Thompson, to locate the first lady. "She's in prison, Mr. President," came the coy reply. "I'm not surprised," replied the president, "but what for?"[50] Eleanor has said she contributed little to her husband's speeches, but those around FDR might beg to differ. Her insightful assessment and candid reports to the president provided firsthand knowledge he might not have gotten otherwise.

Chapter 2

A NEW DEAL FOR THE AMERICAN PEOPLE

The homeless man in this photograph taken at the height of the Great Depression was among the "ill-housed, ill-clad, and ill-nourished" Americans the president hoped to help with the passage of his sweeping New Deal social reforms. (FDR Presidential Library.)

Franklin Roosevelt won a sweeping victory to the White House. But Inauguration Day on March 4, 1933, was a bleak, somber event in Washington, D.C. The cold of that day chilled participants and onlookers to the bone. "This nation, one of history's most promising experiments in democratic living, was foundering on the reefs of economic and social ineptitude," wrote observer Maxwell Meyersohn. In short, America in all her might was dashed on the rocks, scuttled and disenfranchised by the nation's economic crises, the people's hopes further spoiled by the lack of leadership in Washington. Meyersohn wrote that factories, mines, and mills were throwing millions out of work. Bread lines lengthened. Shantytowns pocked the landscape, and small businesses locked their doors—some for good. There were wholesale foreclosures and families living in the streets. Bankers were awaking to find their fortunes gone; working people, their life savings.[51] Just as the people's faith in democracy was at its lowest point, Roosevelt started restoring their hope, building a trust with Americans through his well-crafted and pointed oratory. Gradually, Roosevelt dovetailed words of courage and optimism into his speeches and addresses, thus inspiring the populace to back his New Deal initiatives. "The only thing we have to fear

> **I see one-third of a nation ill-housed, ill-clad, and ill-nourished. The test of our progress is not whether we add more to the abundance of those who have much; it is whether we provide enough for those who have too little.**
>
> *Second inaugural address, Washington, D.C., January 20, 1937.*

is fear itself—nameless, unreasoning, unjustified terror which paralyzes needed efforts to convert retreat into advance," he had said at his inauguration.

Before his election, FDR had pledged himself to a New Deal for the American public. To turn the tide of America's decline, he carried forward that New Deal, first declaring a banking holiday and reorganizing the Federal Reserve System. By strengthening banking structure, banks were able to reopen their doors with new security and minimum loss of depositories.

The first one hundred days of Roosevelt's presidency were a whirlwind. Two days after taking office, on March 6, 1933, he told a conference of governors visiting the White House, "The federal government does have to keep anybody from starving, but the federal

On June 8, 1934, President Franklin D. Roosevelt, in a message to the Congress, announced his intention to provide a program for Social Security. Subsequently, the president created by Executive Order the Committee on Economic Security, which was composed of Secretary of Labor Frances Perkins, Secretary of the Treasury Henry Morgenthau Jr., Secretary of Agriculture Henry A. Wallace, Attorney General Homer S. Cummings, and Federal Emergency Relief Administrator Harry L. Hopkins. The committee was instructed to study the entire problem of economic insecurity and to make recommendations that would serve as the basis for legislative consideration by the Congress. "We can never insure one hundred percent of the population against one-hundred percent of the hazards and vicissitudes of life," said President Roosevelt on August 14, 1935. "But we have tried to frame a law which will give some measure of protection to the average citizen and to his family against the loss of a job and against poverty-ridden old age. This law, too, represents a cornerstone in a structure, which is being built, but is by no means complete. . . . It is . . . a law that will take care of human needs and at the same time provide for the United States an economic structure of vastly greater soundness." The president signed the Social Security Bill into law that day (shown here) as members of his Committee on Economic Security and members of Congress look on. Watching Roosevelt sign are (left to right): Representative Frank H. Buck (D-CA), Representative Robert L. Doughton (D-NC), Senator Alben W. Barkley (D-KY), Senator Robert F. Wagner (D-NY), Representative John D. Dingell (D-MI), Secretary Frances Perkins, Representative Samuel B. Hill (D-WA), and Representative David J. Lewis (D-MD). (Author's collection.)

government should not be called upon to exercise that duty until other agencies fail." During his first fireside chat as president, delivered on March 12, FDR smiled broadly and said: "I can assure you that it is safer to keep your money in a re-opened bank than under the mattress." He spoke candidly of America's predicament with the banks, providing a clearer picture for the average American citizen. After explaining the issue with the banks, and noting banks would reopen the following day, he said, in part, "It is my belief that hoarding during the past week has become an exceedingly unfashionable pastime." He would emphasize this point repeatedly. The next day he explained that the hoarding to which he'd referred in his chat were depositors who took their money out, usually in gold, so it could be stored away no matter what happened to American currency. FDR was acutely aware that these gold hoarders were the same group of what he called "money changers" who'd helped bring on the Great Depression. The Federal Reserve, at the behest of the president, dealt this group a great blow when it asked its member banks to prepare a list of people who withdrew gold or gold certificates from Reserve banks and the U.S. Treasury. When the banks reopened, as promised, on March 13, the public deposited a great deal of money. During his second fireside chat of May 7, 1933, he explained what had happened in banking since his first chat, and he told the public about additional steps being taken to get people working and productive. These measures included the new Civilian Conservation Corps (CCC), the proposed Tennessee Valley Authority (TVA), legislation to save homes and farms from foreclosure, direct unemployment relief appropriations, a proposed public works program, farm relief, the railroad bill, the action on gold, and the international money and disarmament conferences then being held by ministers from overseas.[52] All of these subjects, noted Judge Rosenman, were crowded into a half-hour speech, and were summed up by the president as "a wise and sensible beginning." By 1934, there were few traces left of the fear and panic that once held a tight grip on the nation.

One year into his first term, Franklin Roosevelt authored a book—*On Our Way*—which explicated the guiding principles of the New Deal. "Apart from phrases and slogans," wrote the president, "the important thing to remember is, I think, that the change

> **I never forget that I live in a house owned by all the American people and that I have been given their trust.**
>
> *Fireside chat on economic conditions, Washington, D.C., April 14, 1938.*

in our policy is based upon a change in the attitude and the thinking of the American people—in other words, that it is based on the growing into maturity of our democracy; that it proceeds in accordance with the underlying principles that guided the framers of our Constitution."[53] FDR noted the importance of the people's approval of his New Deal, and that his sweeping economic and social programs were executed with the constant assurance to the people that if at any time they wished to revert to the old methods that his administration had discarded, the public was wholly free to bring about such a reversion by the simple means of the ballot box. An ancient Greek, said Roosevelt, was everlastingly right when he said, "Creation is the victory of persuasion and not of force."[54] The New Deal, he concluded, "seeks that kind of victory."

The president often referenced the U.S. Constitution. When he moved to help impoverished farmers and provide home-owners loans and relaxed credit requirements, he said, "Although it is not written in the Constitution, it is the duty of the federal government to keep its citizens from starvation,"[55] a point he repeated frequently during his speaking engagements the first year of the presidency. But he wasn't without his detractors, particularly when he had substantial powers to enroll workers in federal projects passed to his office. Anti–New Deal proponents, primarily corporate America, wanted the courts to block the New Deal program. The first major challenge to his authority to pull workers into New Deal employment programs involved provisions of

To promote the benefits of Social Security, the new Social Security Administration produced posters to promote its benefits to those it assessed were most likely to qualify for assistance. In the event an insured worker died, his dependent wife and children would be covered by monthly benefits, the children until they reached the age of eighteen (left), and in another, a widow or aged parent (right) might be eligible for spousal benefits. (FDR Presidential Library.)

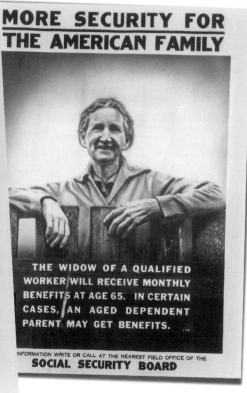

MORE SECURITY FOR THE AMERICAN FAMILY

WHEN AN INSURED WORKER DIES, LEAVING DEPENDENT CHILDREN AND A WIDOW, BOTH MOTHER AND CHILDREN RECEIVE MONTHLY BENEFITS UNTIL THE LATTER REACH 18.

FOR INFORMATION WRITE OR CALL AT THE NEAREST FIELD OFFICE OF THE
SOCIAL SECURITY BOARD

MORE SECURITY FOR THE AMERICAN FAMILY

THE WIDOW OF A QUALIFIED WORKER WILL RECEIVE MONTHLY BENEFITS AT AGE 65. IN CERTAIN CASES, AN AGED DEPENDENT PARENT MAY GET BENEFITS. ...

FOR INFORMATION WRITE OR CALL AT THE NEAREST FIELD OFFICE OF THE
SOCIAL SECURITY BOARD

When Roosevelt sent a message to Congress asking for the power to create the Civilian Conservation Corps (CCC), he envisaged providing jobs for unemployed and unmarried young men between the ages of seventeen and twenty-three who were American citizens. Upon establishment of the CCC, the Labor Department set up a mechanism to recruit prospective young men within three days. The U.S. Army followed suit, calling for its reserve officers to come in and run the camps, and the Forestry Service and National Park Service began to formulate plans and programs—useful projects—for CCC recruits to work on. When complaints about the CCC's soviet-like organization came rolling into the White House, Roosevelt said, "Oh, that doesn't matter. The Army and the Forestry Service will really run the show. The Secretary of Labor will select the men and make the rules and [Robert] Fechner [CCC director] will 'go along' and give everybody satisfaction and confidence."[3] The first CCC camp was established in Virginia on April 17, 1933. Here, Eleanor Roosevelt (seated at the head of the picnic table) visits a CCC camp in Yosemite, California, in 1941. (FDR Presidential Library.)*

the National Industrial Recovery Act which conferred on the president the power to prohibit the transportation in interstate commerce of petroleum that had been produced in excess of the quantity allowed by respective state laws. The Supreme Court's decision, rendered on January 7, 1935, called the act unconstitutional as a delegation of legislative power to the office of the president of the United States. While FDR had beaten his opposition in congressional elections in 1934, the Supreme Court, according to Rosenman, began in 1935 to take the president's programs apart by judicial decisions. Roosevelt continued to press the New Deal forward, however, despite occasional setbacks in the media, courts, and Congress.

Some of the New Deal's greatest victories, in fact, often landed the president in hot water that usually followed a speech in which he used, often against the advice of his speechwriters, anecdotal tidbits on controversial subjects. In a speech to the Alabama Polytechnic Institute, he told a story he knew from the start could be taken one of two ways by his supporters or detractors. But he took the risk and told it anyway. "I had an experience that did not go quite so well with the University of Alabama," he told his audience. "Two years before, the president of the university came to Washington to thank me very much for some PWA [Public Works Administration] money that had been allocated for two dormitories to replace the old dormitories that were unsafe. The law at that time provided that we could use these grants only to aid state institutions to replace buildings that had fallen down or were burned down." He paused. "The president of the university thanked me for the dormitories but, with tears in his eyes, said, 'Mr. President, why didn't you give us the new library too?' I said, 'But the application did not say anything about an old library which had either fallen down or burned down.' He said, 'Mr. President, our library did burn down.' I said, 'When?' And he said, 'In '64. General [William Tecumseh] Sherman came our way.' I believe we stretched the point and went back three-quarters of a century to the date of the arson, and gave him a new library."[56] The crowd roared with laughter. But back in Washington, the president's constant opposition got ammunition it would use to accuse him of misappropriating public works money to curry his popularity in the South. Yet the president's humor was truly an infection of the spirit rather than a forceful play on words. He enjoyed quips and yarns that elicited laughter before large audiences and the press. He enjoyed his humor in private, too.

Sam Rosenman had been all but out of the president's inner circle for the majority of his first term, but that changed a few days before the Democratic National Convention, the president's appearance scheduled for June 27, 1936. He got a call from Marguerite LeHand telling him the president wanted him to stay at the White House during the convention period. While he'd been in town occasionally during the first term, it had always

been for social reasons. This time the president wanted his old friend to lead the crafting of his acceptance speech—nothing had yet been mentioned about helping draft the party platform. It was already no secret that the first draft of the platform on which FDR had run for reelection was prepared by the White House and not the convention.

The CCC did not challenge prevailing racial segregation laws, thus interaction between blacks and whites was curtailed. Color didn't matter as men of color were separated from their white counterparts in the CCC's corps areas, operated by the Department of War, which invoked military camp life and discipline to control productivity and project schedules. An encampment of "colored veterans" is shown here making furniture in the CCC Third Corps camp at Yorktown, Virginia, in 1933, shortly after the establishment of camps in the commonwealth. Some thirty thousand young black men and war veterans, one-tenth of the total CCC enrollment, actively participated in the Civilian Conservation Corps, according to The CCC and Colored Youth, *published by the Roosevelt administration in 1941. (FDR Presidential Library.)*

The Civilian Conservation Corps built a road along the Salmon River from North Fork to Riggins, Idaho, in the 1930s, while its camp youth became heavily involved in forestry, animal husbandry, and agriculture in the adjacent Salmon National Forest. CCC boys from Camp F-167 (shown here) are poised to transplant beaver from a ranch where the beavers were damaging crops to a forest watershed location where they would help conserve the water supply. The picture was taken in 1938. (FDR Presidential Library.)

After some negotiation, party platforms were gradually worked into the equation for the sake of reelection support. From Rosenman's vast experience drafting platforms, he knew that the large assembled group at the White House couldn't possibly get a document drafted expeditiously. Knowing that they were never going to make any headway on the platform with so many hands in the process, William C. Bullitt, now a presidential aide and speechwriter, nominated Rosenman to work through the night getting a draft on paper. The president agreed and the meeting broke up quickly. Rosenman produced a first draft ready for Roosevelt's perusal with his breakfast the following morning. Unfortunately, this first draft of the platform met the same fate that befell subsequent platforms produced by the White House. Many provisions were inserted at the request of various interest groups and convention delegates. After all, the platform should truly be drafted by the convention and not the White House or the candidate, remarked Rosenman later, "provided, of course, that it does not conflict with the candidate's own views."[57]

Having finished his work on the Democratic platform, FDR turned Rosenman's attention to his acceptance speech, the real purpose in his coming back to Washington. FDR's 1936 acceptance speech attacked the reactionaries of the nation, whom he called in the speech,

I propose to create a Civilian Conservation Corps to be used in simple work, more important, however, than the material gains will be the moral and spiritual value of such work.

Message to Congress on unemployment relief, Washington, D.C., March 21, 1933

"economic royalists." These economic royalists, he said, were trying to block economic equality for the average American citizen while the New Deal was "committed to the proposition that freedom is no half-and-half affair. If the average citizen is guaranteed equal opportunity in the polling place, he must have equal opportunity in the market place." The term *economic royalist* was suggested by the president's advisor, Stanley High. In his acceptance speech, he again recognized the rising tide of dictators in Europe and Asia, and of the oppressed people who have "grown too weary to carry on the fight. They have sold their heritage of freedom for the illusion of a living. They have yielded their democracy." He continued, "We are fighting to save a great and precious form of government for ourselves and for the world. This generation of Americans has a rendezvous with destiny," a line that has attached immortality to FDR. "Rendezvous with destiny," said Rosenman, "is another famous phrase which has come down through the years. It was suggested by Tom Corcoran."[58]

The Federal Theater Project (FTP) was one of four—later five—arts projects established within the New Deal's Works Progress Administration (WPA) in 1935, and known altogether as Federal Project Number One. The objective of the FTP was to organize and produce theatrical works, including those in its Children's Theater Units. The FTP was a relief to the many theater professionals who had suffered through the Great Depression, but also from the public's increasing interest in radio and talking motion pictures. The Emperor's New Clothes was the subject of the production shown here, organized and produced by the New York Children's Theater Unit in the FTP's 1935–36 inaugural season. (FDR Presidential Library.)

Eleanor Roosevelt's contribution to the New Deal was the National Youth Administration (NYA), which she helped establish in June 1935. The NYA assisted more than 2 million high school and college students stay in school by giving them grants in exchange for work. Many of these young people worked in libraries and college laboratories, and on agricultural preserves. The NYA also found jobs for about 2.5 million young people who were not in school and not working, including women and minorities. An NYA-sponsored rhythm band played for a public event in the heartland of America: Sandwich, Illinois, in 1936. (FDR Presidential Library.)

The force of falling water becomes electric power in this January 1937 photograph of the Norris Dam. The dam mitigated the disastrous flood that took place also in January 1937, when TVA engineers raised the dam's fourteen-foot steel drum gates for the first time to impound waters that would have swelled a flood more than six hundred miles away along the already swollen Ohio and Mississippi Rivers. Norris Dam has the largest flood control storage of any TVA dam on a tributary of the Tennessee—at normal maximum pool the reservoir holds 2,040,000 acre-feet of water. (FDR Presidential Library.)

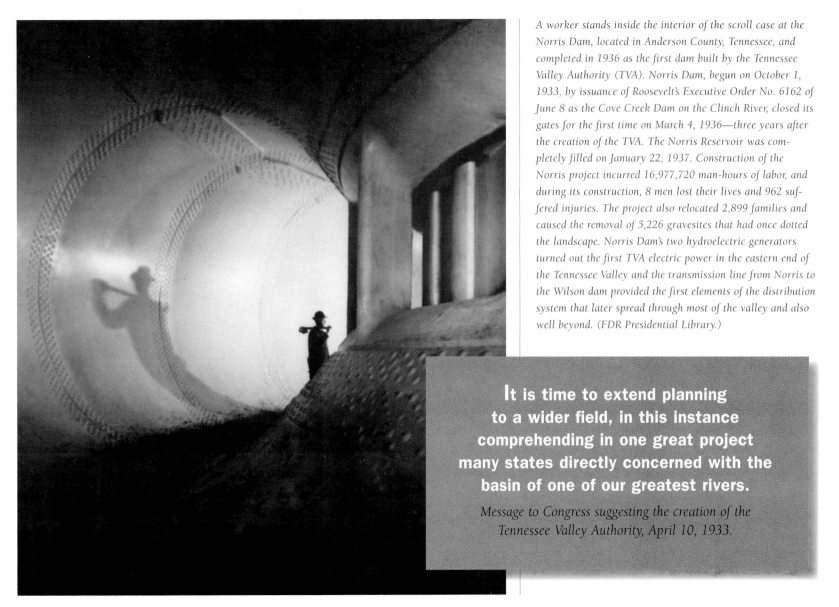

A worker stands inside the interior of the scroll case at the Norris Dam, located in Anderson County, Tennessee, and completed in 1936 as the first dam built by the Tennessee Valley Authority (TVA). Norris Dam, begun on October 1, 1933, by issuance of Roosevelt's Executive Order No. 6162 of June 8 as the Cove Creek Dam on the Clinch River, closed its gates for the first time on March 4, 1936—three years after the creation of the TVA. The Norris Reservoir was completely filled on January 22, 1937. Construction of the Norris project incurred 16,977,720 man-hours of labor, and during its construction, 8 men lost their lives and 962 suffered injuries. The project also relocated 2,899 families and caused the removal of 5,226 gravesites that had once dotted the landscape. Norris Dam's two hydroelectric generators turned out the first TVA electric power in the eastern end of the Tennessee Valley and the transmission line from Norris to the Wilson dam provided the first elements of the distribution system that later spread through most of the valley and also well beyond. (FDR Presidential Library.)

It is time to extend planning to a wider field, in this instance comprehending in one great project many states directly concerned with the basin of one of our greatest rivers.

Message to Congress suggesting the creation of the Tennessee Valley Authority, April 10, 1933.

KEEP ROOSEVELT IN THE WHITE HOUSE

© C. P. CO.

FDR's 1936 campaign for reelection elicited a wide array of political buttons, posters, and paraphernalia, including both of these campaign postcards. "Keep Roosevelt in the White House" read this colorful postcard image (above) from the election, while the "Our Quarterback" postcard has the president's head superimposed on a quarterback's body. (Author's collection.)

Our Quarterback

There are few close-up photographs of Franklin D. Roosevelt addressing Congress. These January 3, 1940, images are rare views of Roosevelt, far less common than wide-angle photographs of the president speaking to the joint house. The pictures shown here are a succession of images that show the president at alternate, animated moments during the same speech. The speech clearly had lighter moments (far left), the president smiling broadly during his speech in the packed congressional chamber. He pauses (center) in his address to the Seventy-sixth Congress to drink from a tumbler of water. Although spectators jammed the chamber and the world at large hung on his words, at times it became dry business for Roosevelt. But in the last frame, the president laughed heartily (near left) during a lighter moment toward the end of the address. His plea for national unity and his serious pledge to keep America out of the growing European conflict had its lighter moments—those which brought laughter from the crowded chamber. (Acme Newspictures. Author's collection.)

Chapter 3

THE GREAT ARSENAL OF DEMOCRACY

For the remainder of the 1936 campaign, the vast majority of FDR's speeches were fairly innocuous. Tom Corcoran, Benjamin Cohen, William Bullitt, and Stanley High worked on them, either alone or in concert with one another. But one of them, the president's speech at Chautauqua, New York, on August 14, was by far the most significant—"the forerunner," observed Sam Rosenman, "of many that he was to make a few years later."[59]

The Chautauqua speech reflected the president's growing concern with events abroad. A clear crisis was shaping that had all the makings for another world war, and since the president had seen a war of global magnitude, this troubled him deeply. Prophetically, he would tell the American people, "We are not isolationists except in so far as we seek to isolate ourselves completely from war. Yet we must remember that so long as war exists on earth there will be some danger that even the nation which most ardently desires peace may be drawn into war." The keynote of this speech, perhaps of FDR's entire foreign policy before Pearl Harbor, were these words: "I have seen war. I have seen war on land and sea. I have seen blood running from the wounded. I have seen men coughing out their gassed lungs. I have seen the dead in the mud. . . . I have seen children starving. I have seen the agony of mothers and wives. I hate war." The speech was a bid to have other nations of the world help the United States maintain world peace— but in that regard the speech was wholly unsuccessful.

The draft of the "I hate war" speech was prepared by William Bullitt. Bullitt told Rosenman the "I hate war" phrase was one he had carried in his memory since 1917. During a private talk with President Woodrow Wilson, soon after the declaration of war

> **W**e must scrupulously guard the civil rights and civil liberties of all our citizens, whatever their background. We must remember that any oppression, any injustice, any hatred, is a wedge designed to attack our civilization.
>
> *Greeting to the American Committee for the Protection of the Foreign Born, Washington, D.C., January 9, 1940.*

by the United States, Wilson, with tears in his eyes, had dramatically seized Bullitt's hands and, with great emotion, used that phrase.[60] The passion and power of the president's observations of war in this speech, which he felt was one of his most important, were those of his predecessor, not FDR himself. With Bullitt's words, with Wilson's observations of his own experience during World War I, FDR crafted one of the most powerful speeches of his presidency.

While the president's first inaugural speech was widely touted as his best, the second, delivered on January 20, 1937, (the inauguration was moved up from March to close the gap between the presidential election and the swearing in) was of equal quality and candor. Donald Richberg submitted the first draft of a complete speech, which became the basis of the first draft for the president. Rosenman completed the second, a summation of the president's thoughts, called the "I see" comments, of the speech. Though Rosenman tried to rein in the president's string of "I see" comments, FDR took one look at what he'd done and crossed out everything after the final "I see" and scribbled: "I see one-third of a nation ill-housed, ill-clad, ill-nourished." In the end, this speech was as big a hit with the public as his first. "I see a great nation, upon a great continent, blessed with a great wealth of natural resources," he told the people. Reading the speech years later in the Roosevelt Presidential Library at Hyde Park, Sam Rosenman noticed it was all wrinkled from being exposed to the driving rain on inaugural day. But mostly, and amusingly, he noticed how much attention the president had paid to his delivery, carefully going over his speeches beforehand to make sure his reading would be correct. In reading one draft of the speech, Rosenman noticed that FDR had transposed the "head" and the "heart" in a

FDR sent greetings to a gathering of the American Committee for the Protection of the Foreign Born (ACPFB) in Washington, D.C., on January 9, 1940. He said: "We must scrupulously guard the civil rights and civil liberties of all our citizens, whatever their background. We must remember that any oppression, any injustice, any hatred, is a wedge designed to attack our civilization." The faces of this Native American, possibly Mexican-born, father and his children stare wide-eyed into the camera in an image that was taken in the early 1900s. But they are indicative of the citizenry President Roosevelt targeted in New Deal reforms. Interestingly, Roosevelt did not appear before the ACPFB in person, providing himself distance from an organization perceived as an overly progressive civil liberties organization or a Communist front, or both, depending on which view of the ACPFB was true. (Author's collection.)

The president delivered one of his most important pre-World War II speeches at Chautauqua, New York, on August 14, 1936. The speech, popularly known as the "I hate war" address, served as the keynote of Roosevelt's foreign policy in the long years before the Japanese attack on Pearl Harbor. "I have seen war. I have seen war on land and sea. I have seen blood running from the wounded. I have seen the dead in the mud. I have seen cities destroyed. I have seen children starving. I have seen the agony of mothers and wives. I hate war." Though a direct bid for nations around the world to join the United States in its efforts to maintain peace, the speech was unsuccessful. William C. Bullitt, one of the president's long-time speechwriters, wrote the draft of the speech. Bullitt told Sam Rosenman that the phrase "I hate war" was one he had carried in his memory since 1917. "During a private talk with President [Woodrow] Wilson soon after the declaration of war by the United States, Wilson, with tears in his eyes, had dramatically seized Bullitt's hands and, in great emotion, had used that phrase."[4] President Roosevelt felt that this was one of his most important speeches and had it printed up the following Christmas as a brochure, shown here, which he typically inscribed to friends who received one. (Author's collection.)

PEACE

★

President Franklin D. Roosevelt's
Speech at Chautauqua,
New York

AUGUST 14, 1936

"I hate war"

sentence. To make sure he wouldn't confuse the two as he delivered the speech, he drew a head above the "head" and heart with an arrow through it over the "heart."[61]

In the years that intervened before World War II, FDR made what Sam Rosenman later called "a full dress comparison between our democracy and the concept of government held by the rulers of German, Italy, Russia, and Japan. Although he didn't mention them by name in several speeches, it was more than clear to the American people who he was talking about."[62] He continued to sound the alarm that world conflict was gradually building to a crescendo, and could not be ignored much longer. In the "quarantine" speech delivered at Chicago on October 5, 1937, Roosevelt spoke solely of foreign affairs. The speech caused a sensation and was largely condemned as warmongering and saber rattling by the United States. One telegram sent by an angry citizen to the White House stated, "If you hate war do not try to incite it by such appeals as that you made on the 5th in Chicago," while another went on, "All right if you want peace keep the peace. No one is coming over here to attack us."[63] Despite its critics, the "quarantine" speech was a milestone in the foreign policy of the United States: It was Roosevelt's first attempt to stoke support for collective security instead of isolationism and blind neutrality. Rosenman believes Roosevelt's mistake was in trying to bring the American public along too fast to this switch in policy. The next day, at a well-attended press conference, he pulled back from his position with the intention of going out on a limb more slowly on the next attempt to broach collective security with the public—and by then, an attentive world community.

By 1940 Roosevelt had begun asking for more national defense funding from Congress, and on June 10 of that year, the day Italy entered the war in Europe on the side of Germany, he made an address at the University of Virginia. The State Department prepared the speech he had in hand, White House staff having had noth-

FDR greets Illinois National Guardsmen circa 1935 with future Army Chief of Staff, then-Colonel George C. Marshall seated next to him in the car. Between 1933 and 1936, Marshall was in Chicago as senior instructor to the Illinois National Guard, sent there by Army Chief of Staff General Douglas A. MacArthur, largely viewed by Marshall's biographers as the bane of Marshall's existence and the one person preventing the colonel from becoming a general.

ing to do with its crafting. On the way down to Charlottesville, he inserted in his own hand a sentence that dramatically illustrated Italy's entry into the war, thus dramatizing an event already sending shock waves through the international community. "On this tenth day of June, 1940, the hand that held the dagger has struck it into the back of its neighbor," he'd scribbled on the paper in front of him. This speech came to be known as the "stab-in-the-back" speech, the president's words borrowed from a cable sent to him that morning by French Premier Paul Reynaud. Sumner Welles, who thought better of the president using it, had initially removed the phrase from FDR's reading copy. But FDR put it back on his way to Virginia.

The president broke a great precedent by running for a third term in 1940. From the beginning of that summer to Election Day, FDR was on the campaign trail, pursuing an office that had had no third term tradition. William Bullitt, who had worked on speeches for the president from 1933 on when he was in the United States, proved particularly helpful crafting Roosevelt's speeches in the summer and fall of 1940. But he liked to

President Roosevelt was urged to refurbish the guard by creating a national network of armories politically camouflaged as community centers, modeled after Marshall's revamping of the Illinois Guard program. Marshall's allies, especially General John J. "Black Jack" Pershing, used Marshall's Illinois accomplishments to lobby Roosevelt for his promotion. Marshall was promoted to brigadier general in October 1936 and given command of Vancouver Barracks, Washington, and its CCC district from 1936-38. His ascent was thereafter assured. FDR named Marshall Army Chief of Staff in 1939, a position he held until his "retirement" in November 1945. (Author's collection.)

work alone and was never a part of the full writing team. Bullitt's preferred distance from the team—and thereby the president—eventually caused an irreparable rift with the White House the following year, and so ended Bullitt's contributions to FDR's oratory.

After finishing an important campaign speech in Boston on October 30, 1940, one that touched upon America's possible involvement—in the event of attack—in the unfolding war in Europe, Roosevelt was on the home stretch with a rapid succession of speeches left before elections. For many days prior to his delivery of the speech in Boston, political leaders begged him to bring comfort to the nation's mothers that their sons, if drafted for war, would be fed and quartered properly. FDR thought about Edward J. Flynn, boss of New York's Bronx borough and former head of the Democratic Party. Ed Flynn had one rule about any political speech: It should contain some mention of mothers. He'd telegraphed the president more than once that the president should include mothers in his speech. His reasoning was quite simple: "Everybody has them, and you ought to be for them." In the speech, FDR went back and inserted a mention of mothers and wired Flynn: "Speech finished. Listen in tonight. 'Mother' is finally in."[64]

Roosevelt's December 29, 1940, fireside chat was one of his most impactful. This was his famous "arsenal of democracy" speech. Sherwood and Rosenman contributed heavily to "the arsenal of democracy" speech. Hopkins also joined in. The speech's most important statement, "We must be the great arsenal of democracy. . . . No dictator, no combination of dictators, will weaken that determination by threats of how they will construe that determination," was the president coaxing the public closer to the reality of war. The phrase "arsenal of democracy," which appeared for the first time in this speech, was actually coined by the French representative then in Washington, Jean Monnet. Monnet used the phrase in late 1940 in a conversation with Justice Frankfurter to describe the most effective assistance the United States could provide in a world struggling against tyranny.[65] Frankfurter passed it along to the president as well as to Assistant Secretary of War John J. McCloy, who submitted it in a draft speech from the War Department. In the speech Roosevelt delivered, containing this key phrase, the president presented a long-range plan of action for the nation, one based largely on strengthening

> **We must be the great arsenal of democracy.**
>
> *Fireside chat on national security, Washington, D.C., December 29, 1940.*

President Roosevelt embarked the Portland-class cruiser Indianapolis (CA-35), flagship of Scouting Force 1, on November 17, 1936, at Charleston, South Carolina, for a good-neighbor cruise to South America. After carrying President Roosevelt to Rio de Janeiro, Buenos Aires, and Montevideo for state visits, she returned to Charleston on December 15, where the presidential party left the ship. The picture shown here was taken on November 17. (FDR Presidential Library.)

The USS New Mexico *(BB-40), the lead ship of its class, first commissioned on May 20, 1918, was modernized and overhauled at the Philadelphia Navy Yard in the early thirties before being returned to the Pacific Fleet to resume training exercises and tactical development operations in October 1934. President Roosevelt embarked aboard* New Mexico *during one of her fleet problem exercises off the coast of California, likely on the tail end of the president's trip to the Pacific Coast that had begun September 22, 1937, at Hyde Park. The president's fondness for the U.S. Navy was apparent throughout his presidency, but it is likely that his visit to* New Mexico *—to the fleet itself—was FDR immersing himself in America's military might before delivering one of his most controversial speeches on the return leg of his trip. The "quarantine" speech was give at Chicago on October 5, 1937. When Samuel I. Rosenman asked Under Secretary of State Sumner Welles what he thought of the speech, he said, "At that time he [Roosevelt] was, I think, more immediately concerned with the situation in the Pacific than with conditions in Europe. As you undoubtedly remember, he was talking with the Navy about drawing an actual line in the Pacific to be maintained by the United States, if the British would agree to cooperate . . . ."[5] The president used the word quarantine in connection with that line in the Pacific. Roosevelt is seated on the deck of* New Mexico, *surrounded by five of her crew, one of whom is (far right) Aviation Machinist's Mate First Class (AMM1c) Lorence N. Bredahl of Fontanelle, Iowa. The photograph belonged to Bredahl, who kept it in a chronologically arranged album documenting his naval career—and the president's visit. (Author's collection.)*

the country's defensive posture. A year later, however, he had to tell the American people the country was at war. His fireside chat of December 9, 1941, referenced previously, was deadly serious, direct and clear. "We are now in this war," he told the nation, "We are all in it—all the way." His last fireside chat, was delivered on June 12, 1944, six days after the Allies stormed the beachhead at Normandy, the beginning of Europe's liberation from the tyranny of German dictator Adolf Hitler.

When inauguration day came in January 1941, Franklin Delano Roosevelt stood in a position where no man before—or since—could claim he'd been—being sworn into his third term of office as president of the United States. He was, in the opinion of many of his closest advisors, at the summit of his political power as he took his third oath of office. His fireside chat of December 29, 1940, and his third inaugural address, in particular, reached heights that arguably he never again attained for the remainder of his presidency. His third inaugural address, "so vital, so compact, so intellectually masterful, and so eloquent with the faith that was in him that any account of the wisdom with which he endowed his administration demands that it be read in full. In any time of peril to this nation," wrote Frank Kingdon, who first met the president in his third term "its citizens may return to this document and it will sustain them."[66] Like many of the most important addresses Roosevelt was to make in his twelve years in the White House, quotes from this address are not reflected in the inscriptions in the FDR Memorial in the nation's capital.

"Lives of nations are determined not by the count of years, but by the lifetime of the human spirit. The life of a man is three score years and ten: a little more, a little less. The life of a nation is the fullness of the measure of its will to live," he told the throngs gathered for his inaugural. "A nation, like a person, has something deeper, something more permanent, something larger than the sum of all its parts. It is something, which matters most to its future—which calls forth the most sacred guarding of its present. It is a thing

for which we find it difficult, even impossible, to hit upon a single, simple word. And yet, we all understand what it is— the spirit—the faith of America."

Four years later he would be more brief—552 words. It has been described as the speech of a man in labor, hoping to bring peace to a war-torn world. "In the days and the years that are to come, we shall work for a just and honorable peace, a durable peace, as today we work and fight for total victory in war. We can and we will achieve," he continued, "such a peace." But to forge a lasting peace, Roosevelt had to get the great arsenal of democracy through four years of hell on the battlefield. The Second World War was a test of his leadership—and of his personal

President Roosevelt, pictured here at the White House on December 8, 1941—the morning after the Japanese attack on Pearl Harbor—had been up most of the night before crafting his declaration of war speech to be delivered before a joint session of Congress. Many of the actions taken by Roosevelt on December 7, post-Japanese attack, required the president to sign an Executive Order. The president instructed his staff to go ahead and execute whatever needed to be done and he would sign the order later. The president, depicted here, signed the order that permitted him the latitude to order the Japanese embassy and all the consulates in the United States protected and ordered all Japanese citizens to be picked up and placed under surveillance. The Department of Justice concurred with the president's order. Roosevelt also ordered that guards be placed not only on all military-run arsenals but also on all private munitions factories and all bridges. He refused to have military guards posted around the White House. (FDR Presidential Library.)

On December 11, 1941, FDR sent a message to Congress that Germany and Italy, pursuing a course of world conquest, had declared war against the United States. "The long-known and the long-expected," wrote the president, "has thus taken place. The forces endeavoring to enslave the entire world now are moving toward this hemisphere." The war resolution that came down from the U.S. House of Representatives and Senate, and signed by the president (shown here) gave Roosevelt the authority to employ the entire naval and military forces of the government to carry on war against Germany, and to bring the conflict to a successful termination using any and all resources of the country to do it. (Library of Congress. Author's collection.)

strength of character. FDR was, in the final analysis, for all his foibles—and there were quite a few—a thoughtful and caring man. He was so thoughtful in his third and into his fourth terms that he often extended great kindness to his friends and closest advisors, even after their deaths. FDR began to lose many of those closest to him during the third and fourth terms, often burying them from the White House, a formality that he insisted upon for Louis Howe, whom Frank Kingdon called FDR's "best, bravest, and most intelligent friend he ever had."[67]

Roosevelt also delighted in press conferences during the war years, which he'd used throughout his presidency to strengthen the public's bond to him—and vice versa. The public's image of Roosevelt during this period was classic: Roosevelt tilting his cigarette holder and exchanging lively banter with the press corps, and nearly always after a headline. But then, he was so skilled at handling the press, he came across as confident and assured, no matter what the headline screamed. He was a masterful actor, expressive, it being not so much what he said but how he said it.

The war years brought FDR the man into his full prime. He was powerful and by far the leader among leaders who made up the "Big Three"—FDR, Winston S. Churchill of Great Britain, and Joseph Stalin of the Soviet Union. And Churchill and Stalin would concur that he was the spirit of their alliance—the heart of victory when it came in late 1945. But in these years, FDR also reached the pinnacle of his popularity with the public, and the public saw the full measure of the man in the White House's humor—and candor—with the people.

During the war, one of his problems was Madame Chiang, wife of Generalissimo Chiang Kai-Shek of China, someone Frank Kingdon described as "a fascinating combination of outward grace and inward ruthlessness." FDR saw both in the "Missimo," who'd sought her access to the president through Eleanor, whom she'd endeared herself to,

> **W**e have faith that future generations will know that here, in the middle of the twentieth century, there came a time when men of good will found a way to unite, and produce, and fight to destroy the forces of ignorance, and intolerance, and slavery, and war.
>
> *Address to the White House Correspondents' Association, Washington, D.C., February 12, 1943.*

Planning for an adequate home-grown food supply brought this New York woman, as it did to hundreds of thousands of Americans like her, a realization of the economic value of farm-produced food and fuel, and a keener appreciation of the advantages of farm living. Taken in 1942, this woman and her family were just emerging from the lean times of the Great Depression—and the country was facing the stark reality of world war on two fronts. (FDR Presidential Library.)

President Roosevelt's April 10, 1933, address to Congress suggesting legislation to create the Tennessee Valley Authority (TVA), called the Muscle Shoals development "but a small part of the potential usefulness of the entire Tennessee River." The president's subsequent notes, added later to the published congressional message pertaining to the TVA's establishment, stated: "The Tennessee Valley Authority created by this act was established, in the words of the document, '. . . for the purpose of maintaining and operating the properties now owned by the United States in the vicinity of Muscle Shoals, Alabama, in the interest of the national defense and for agricultural and industrial development, and to improve navigation in the Tennessee River and to control the destructive floodwaters in the Tennessee and Mississippi River Basins. . . ." National defense was on the president's mind—as well as the collective conscience of American legislators—eight years before the United States entered World War II. Here, a black worker at Muscle Shoals is pictured tending an electric phosphate-smelting furnace that was producing elemental phosphorus at a TVA chemical plant in June 1942. Phosphatic fertilizer was shipped abroad under provisions of the Lend-Lease Bill. (Photograph by Alfred T. Palmer. Courtesy FDR Presidential Library.)

exposing only her charming persona. But FDR was with Madame only a brief time before he became aware of "the fangs behind the charm." During a dinner Roosevelt began to talk about labor leader John L. Lewis, at the time making headlines with well-publicized labor disputes. FDR asked "Missimo," as he liked to call her, what she would do with Lewis in China. She raised her hand and drew it across her throat in an unmistakable gesture. At his first opportunity afterward, he whispered to Eleanor, "What do you think of your charmer now?"[68]

Other occasions were altogether different. FDR moved around quickly in his wheelchair, sometimes coming upon people unexpectedly. Kingdon recounts one occasion of this, which is now famous, that involved Roosevelt's friend, British Prime Minister Winston Churchill, who was staying at the White House on one of his trips west to consult FDR. Churchill's routine was to rise late, and spend a few hours dictating to his male secretary. "To satisfy his primitive urges," writes Kingdon, "Churchill would often do all this in a state of complete undress." But late one morning, he was startled to have FDR roll into his room unannounced to find him "unadorned except for the inevitable cigar." Churchill, however, was equal to the occasion, saying to the president, "You see, Sir, I have always told you that the prime minister has nothing to conceal from the president of the United

States." Later, Grace Tully caught FDR chuckling to himself and asked him why. He told her—the nice version of the story, of course—"You know, Grace, I just happened to think of it now. He's pink-and-white all over."[69]

Churchill and Roosevelt shared in common their use of the press to foster the public's fervor for victory in the face of a two-front war. They consulted frequently, becoming close friends in the process. Few, if any, of Roosevelt's wartime speeches, observed Rosenman, failed to devote some time and attention to propaganda and its use in rallying the American public—and the troops. He promised heavy attacks by land, sea, and air, the statement of inevitable victory, the message of hope and faith to the people in occupied countries, the triumphant recital of American production figures, and the prospect of human freedoms throughout the postwar world.[70] During a speech to White House correspondents on February 12, 1943, as the tide of war turned in favor of the Allies, he repeated a Roman Orthodox proverb: "It is permitted to you, my children, in time of danger, to walk with the Devil until you have crossed the bridge."[71] During the first and second years of the war, the president knew better than to be overly optimistic with the public, but when the Allies began to experience successive victories in Europe and the Pacific, his tone dramatically changed. Propaganda, certainly; unjustified propaganda, not likely once America entered 1943. While he didn't sugarcoat the fact that war entailed perhaps large casualties in the months, perhaps years, to come, at least he could report that the Allies were winning. At the end of the year, rather than address the nation from Capitol Hill, Roosevelt opted for a fireside chat on Christmas Eve, and tie in the objective of permanent world peace discussed at the Teheran Conference, which had ended less than two weeks before. The president spent a great deal of time on this speech, and it was the eighth draft that was presented from Hyde Park on December 24. This speech of major importance during the war was accorded worldwide coverage by radio and newspapers and also by all the government facilities of the Office of War Information (OWI), because the objective was to have it reach every corner of the world—to encour-

> **They (who) seek to establish systems of government based on the regimentation of all human beings by a handful of individual rulers call this a new order. It is not new and it is not order.**
>
> *Address to the annual dinner for the White House Correspondents' Association, Washington, D.C., March 15, 1941.*

age and strengthen the resolve of those fighting the good fight.

The president's advisors readily realized by 1944 that FDR intended to run for a fourth term. By July that year, Democratic National Committee Chairman Robert E. Hannegan reported that most of the delegates picked for the convention were already pledged to the president. In FDR's mind, the objective of his fourth term was creation of a functioning United Nations organization, which would require the complete cooperation of both Democrats and Republicans in Congress. His last political campaign would present the president with a firestorm of heated domestic and wartime issues.

After an unfortunate experience with his leg braces on the campaign trail in Bremerton, Washington, FDR opted to make his major political campaign speeches sitting down. His braces had become painful, and could not be readjusted to make him comfortable. Speeches delivered during the campaign were subsequently scheduled at dinners or large venues like ballparks, where he could speak from an open automobile and not seem weak or ill to those in attendance. The only time he stood to deliver a speech in the 1944 campaign was as he spoke to a huge crowd from the back of a train at the station. "One day in September," wrote Sam Rosenman, "before he gave up the idea of standing during his speeches, I went into his bedroom and found him with his braces on walking up and down, leaning on the arm of Dr. [Ross] McIntire. He was literally trying to learn to walk again!"[72] The drawback to his sitting during speeches was, obviously, attack from his political opponents. Rumors circulated about his poor health and inability to subsequently withstand the strain of a vigorous political campaign. To dispel any notion he could not stay in the race and win, Roosevelt took deliberate

Wheeler Dam, named for Joseph Wheeler, a Confederate general during the Civil War, was built to make Muscle Shoals a navigable waterway. Before construction of Wheeler and Wilson Dams, and Pickwick Landing, Muscle Shoals beset the portion of the Tennessee River that flowed through Northwest Alabama. The shoals were an impassible stretch of shallow rapids. TVA workers began construction of the dam on November 30, 1933, and finished it nearly three years later, on October 3, 1936, at a cost of $89 million. The completion of Wheeler Dam and other dams in the TVA network increased the water depth so that navigation was feasible along the Tennessee. Wheeler Dam navigation lock, its TVA signage clearly visible, is shown here as it appeared in 1942. (FDR Presidential Library.)

Makeshift housing dotted the rolling hills around Tennessee Valley Authority projects. Here, three barefoot, threadbare children stare back at a photographer tasked to take pictures of the poor stranded in proximity of the old Congress Mine in 1942. (FDR Presidential Library.)

A photographer taking pictures of Tennessee housing for the TVA in 1942 documented the sole water supply in this section of Wilder, Tennessee, located in Fentress County. (FDR Presidential Library.)

steps to make appearances more frequently and greet the public smiling broadly and confidently as he had done in his three previous elections.

But the stress and strain of his office had taken a bitter toll on Roosevelt. The president spoke before the Foreign Policy Association dinner in Washington on October 21, 1944, and shortly afterwards, those in attendance began reporting back to Eleanor that FDR looked ill that night. "But I was not surprised," wrote Eleanor, "because of course he was extremely tired."[73] As the year ended, FDR won an unprecedented fourth term in office and much-needed family time at Warm Springs and, of course, Christmas with his family at Hyde Park.

From the Yalta Conference, which produced the United Nations, in February 1945 until his death that April, it was obvious to Rosenman and the president's closest aides that the fighting eloquence and oratory that distinguished FDR in his successful presidential campaign only four months before was sorely lacking. His ad-libs were off. Roosevelt's ad-libbing about Russia, in particular, didn't usually add to the quality of his speeches he otherwise delivered with satisfactory success. The president's ad-libbing had always been a source of amusement for his speechwriters, but they

always encouraged the president to refrain from doing it in major speeches.

Roosevelt's speechwriters, primarily Sam Rosenman, began drafting a speech for the president to present before Congress on the agreements reached at Yalta. The president worked on initial and later drafts of the address; the fifth draft became the reading copy, "but the president made so many corrections in the reading copy that it was retyped as a sixth draft."[74] Rosenman went up to Capitol Hill to hear him deliver this key report to Congress on March 1, 1945, and to his dismay, the president was halting and ineffective in his presentation. He ad-libbed again, more frequently than Rosenman had ever heard him do. Most of his extemporaneous remarks were, in the judge's opinion, irrelevant, some even ridiculous. He was fighting for the eloquent and masterful oratory that had only months before helped put him back in the White House for his fourth term. But the crushing effect of twelve years in office had become evident in one speech, one very important address that might chart the course of world peace post conflict. Perhaps worse yet, delivering this speech to Congress on the results of the Yalta Conference,

"These are the faces of victory," read the wartime caption of this Office of War Information (OWI) photograph of a riveter, taken in September 1942. "Each day he nourishes the great growing splendor of the TVA. Tomorrow, he and thousands of other workers will see a new plant, harnessed with electrical power to produce the weapons of death of [Adolf] Hitler." The Office of War Information was created in 1942 and served as an important U.S. government propaganda agency during World War II. During 1942 and 1943, the OWI contained two photographic units, the first a section headed by Roy Emerson Stryker and the second the news bureau. (The units were merged during 1943.) The photographers in both units documented America's mobilization during the early years of World War II, concentrating on such topics as aircraft factories and women in the workforce. Stryker's section at the OWI had been transferred from the Department of Agriculture's Farm Security Administration (FSA) in late 1942. The OWI News Bureau operated within the Office for Emergency Management (OEM) during 1941 and 1942. (FDR Presidential Library.)

the president made a major—and rare—mistake in public relations. Roosevelt failed to disclose one of the Yalta agreements. "His decision not to disclose it in his speech was the kind of mistake he had never made before, and I have never been able to understand the reason for it in this case."[75] The president met an onslaught of criticism for his nondisclosure. Haggard and disappointed that Soviet leader Joseph Stalin had begun to beg off agreements at Yalta, Roosevelt retreated to Warm Springs, Georgia, to his "Little White House" to regain his spirits.

I have seen war. I have seen war on land and sea. I have seen blood running from the wounded. I have seen the dead in the mud. I have seen cities destroyed. I have seen children starving. I have seen the agony of mothers and wives. I hate war.

—*Address at Chautauqua, New York, August 14, 1936.*

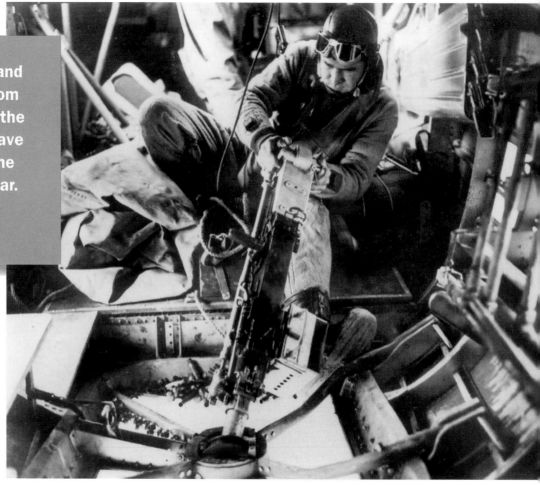

United States Army Air Force gunner Sergeant Williams Watts, of Alexandria, Louisiana, fires his machine gun on the enemy during an aerial engagement with the German Luftwaffe somewhere over Europe in 1942. Watts was part of a bomber crew. (FDR Presidential Library.)

(Left) Roosevelt visited General Dwight D. Eisenhower (seated in the backseat of the president's jeep) and General George S. Patton (standing left) in Castelvetrano, Sicily, to review the troops on December 8, 1943, two years into the war. (FDR Presidential Library.)

(Right) President Roosevelt began the practice of inviting foreign heads of state to the presidential retreat at Shangri-La, located in Maryland's Catoctin Mountains. During World War II, British Prime Minister Winston Churchill made two visits to the retreat. On the second visit, Churchill arrived in Washington on May 11, 1943, to confer with Roosevelt and three days later—on May 14—he accompanied Roosevelt to Shangri-La for a three-day weekend. The photograph shown here was taken on May 14, 1943, the first day of Churchill's visit with Roosevelt. This visit subsequently extended into the following weekend. During the two weekends that encompassed his 1943 visit, Churchill preferred to relax while exploring the hilly countryside of the well-guarded Shangri-La compound. But he occasionally fished with the president, doing more smoking than casting a pole into Little Hunting Creek. Sitting side-by-side on portable canvas chairs, Roosevelt fished and Churchill puffed away on a cigar as the two leaders talked for hours. Shangri-La is today called Camp David. (FDR Presidential Library.)

Chapter 4

MOSES IN THE PROMISED LAND

President Roosevelt signs a deed for the gift of property for his library at Hyde Park in 1939 as Eleanor (left) and Frank C. Walker (right) look on. Roosevelt appointed Walker as chairman of the Democratic Party, and later, postmaster general, a position Walker held from 1940 to 1945. (From Eleanor Roosevelt's This I Remember.*)*

FDR was vacationing at his Little White House in Warm Springs, Georgia, tired from his recent travel abroad with longtime mistress Lucy Mercer Rutherfurd (referred to hereafter as "Mercer") and artist Elizabeth Shoumatoff, who was commissioned by Mercer to paint a portrait of the president. During the president's forty-first visit to his favorite retreat, on the afternoon of April 12, 1945, he was sitting for his portrait for Madame Shoumatoff, making polite conversation and reading some reports as she painted. Without warning, FDR suddenly grabbed his temple with his left hand and slumped backwards into his chair. Shoumatoff leapt up and went for help. Arthur Prettyman, FDR's valet, and Joe Espencilla, his Filipino houseboy, heard the president mutter feebly that he had a terrific headache. Roosevelt died later that afternoon of a massive cerebral hemorrhage. But Mercer and Shoumatoff were long gone. In the chaos that ensued after FDR's collapse, historian Doris Kearns Goodwin wrote that Mercer told Shoumatoff: "We must pack and go. The family is arriving by plane and the rooms must be vacant. We must get to Aiken [South Carolina] before dark."[76] Shortly after 3:30 that afternoon, driving near Macon, Georgia, Mercer leaned over and turned on the car radio. The music stopped midway through the song for an announcement: The president had died.

Word of FDR's collapse first reached Admiral Dr. Ross T. McIntire, one of the president's attending physicians, back in Washington earlier in the afternoon. Eleanor was informed but assured that Dr. Howard G. Bruenn, with the president in Warm Springs, was properly attending her husband. McIntire didn't know just how grim the prognosis had become, and when informed, called Eleanor away from a benefit for the thrift shop at the Sulgrave Club in Washington to the White House, where she was told her husband had fallen gravely ill. "In my heart I knew what had happened, but one does not actually formulate these terrible thoughts until they are spoken,"[77] she wrote later. She withdrew to her sitting room in the White House as Stephen T. Early, the president's press secretary, and Dr. McIntire came in to tell her the news of FDR's cerebral hemorrhage and death. That evening, Early and McIntire accompanied Eleanor by plane to Warm Springs. But before her departure, Eleanor saw her husband's vice president, Harry S. Truman, and cabled her sons: "Father slept away. He would expect you to carry on and finish your jobs."

Those gathered around the dead president at Warm Springs, his doctors and staff, tried to hold back their grief and disbelief. As the news correspondents at Warm Springs scrambled to get the story of FDR's death on the wire, Grace Tully, his secretary, "walked into the bedroom, leaned over, and kissed the president lightly on the forehead."[78] Roosevelt was sixty-three. Eleanor's grief would be altogether something different. Warm Springs was enveloped in heartbreak as staff consoled one another and Eleanor picked herself up to offer them comfort. But there was also heartbreak of the very personal kind, heartbreak for a wife whose husband held out his greatest affection for another woman. When she arrived in Warm Springs, Eleanor quickly discovered that Mercer had been there when FDR was stricken. In his 1966 book, *The Time Between the Wars*, Jonathan Daniels, a former Roosevelt aide and press secretary who later became editor of the Raleigh, North Carolina, *News & Observer*, opined: "Supposedly, he ended forever his relations with Lucy Mercer [a promise FDR made to Eleanor after the original affair was discovered in 1918], to whom actually he was to be attached by ties of deep and unbroken affection to the day he died."[79] Mercer died in 1948 at the age of fifty-seven, but her correspondence to and from FDR, whom she'd loved for nearly three decades, was never found.

On a cold, snowy day in the nation's capital, FDR (center) observes President Abraham Lincoln's birthday at the foot of the Lincoln Memorial on February 12, 1944. First Lady Eleanor Roosevelt stands one over, to the left of the president. Roosevelt was already beginning to show signs of poor health catching up to him. (Author's collection.)

The weight of waging war is reflected in this May 27, 1944, photograph of President Roosevelt as he met with Phyllis Fay Firebagh, daughter of a U.S. veteran. (FDR Presidential Library.)

FDR's body was loaded aboard a presidential train that snaked its way slowly from Warm Springs to Washington, a trip the president knew all too well. "I lay in my berth all night with the window shade up, looking out at the countryside he had loved, and watching the faces of the people at stations and even at the crossroads, who came to pay their last tribute all through the night,"[80] wrote Eleanor. She had, after all, learned to keenly observe the American people through the countless trips by train she'd taken with her husband before and after his first election to the presidency. At the peak of her personal grief, she'd found strength in her relationship with Franklin, sprinkled tenuously with affection but bound together by familiarity and the passage of time. "Men and women who live together through long years get to know one another's failings; but they also come to know what is worthy of respect and admiration in those they live with and in themselves. If at the end one can say: 'This man used to the limit the powers that God granted him; he was worthy of love and respect and of the sacrifices of many people, made in order that he might achieve what he deemed to be his task,' then that life has been lived well and there are no regrets."[81]

Before Eleanor left Washington for Warm Springs to retrieve FDR's body, she had begun, in conference with various family members and the president's closest advisors, to plan his funeral. The funeral train bearing Roosevelt's body arrived in the nation's capital on April 13. Throngs watched as the coffin bearing their president was loaded on a black caisson and taken through the capital's crowded streets to the White House East Room. Three of the

More than an end to war, we want an end to the beginnings of all wars.

Undelivered address prepared for Jefferson Day to have been given on April 13, 1945, from Georgia Hall, Warm Springs, Georgia. President Roosevelt died on April 12.

Roosevelts' four sons missed their father's East Room ceremony; Elliott was the only one who could make it as he'd been asked to fly the plane that brought back Bernard Baruch and Sam Rosenman from London. James arrived after the Hyde Park interment, so he didn't join the family until the train trip from New York back to Washington. Franklin Jr. and John were on duty in the Pacific. On the day of FDR's funeral, Harry Hopkins looked as if he was about to die. The "brain trust" was slowly ebbing away.

Hyde Park was turned over to the federal government, as FDR had wished, on April 12, 1946, one year to the day after his death. President Harry S. Truman attended, but he shared the podium with Eleanor Roosevelt, who told those gathered that Franklin Roosevelt considered the estate, under federal ownership, as a place to which the people of the nation—and even the world—might come to find the same rest, peace and strength Roosevelt himself had derived from his visits there. She had no regrets about turning over Hyde Park to the government for safekeeping. "For one thing," she said, "my children and grandchildren might now learn about their illustrious ancestor in a way that would have been impossible had they lived on in the house. Then, too, it was better to pass on the house with its contents just as it had been left by my husband so that it might not take on any of the personality of those who might have made the house their home after his death."[82] Hyde Park was part of FDR's mystique, his legacy, and as Eleanor observed, "his spirit." "His spirit will always live in this house, in the library and in the rose garden where he wished his grave to be."[83]

Astutely, Eleanor Roosevelt took on the role of preserving her husband's legacy as the nation's longest-serving chief executive. But it was a lonely part to play, both when FDR was alive and after his death. "Readjustments in one's inner life have to go on forever," she wrote as she began to clear out of the main house at Hyde Park and fix up the cottage at Val-Kill as her primary residence. Her major decisions as to how she'd live out the rest of

FDR was stumping for reelection—his fourth term—with a series of important campaign speeches when he arrived the evening of October 28, 1944, in Chicago, having made the journey by presidential train from Philadelphia. On the train between venues, the speech Roosevelt was to deliver at Soldier Field was polished, filling in aspects that had been crafted before the president and his advisers left Washington on the campaign trail. Several drafts were presented to FDR, as there hadn't been enough time in Washington to check it carefully. "The Chicago speech is one of the few of which any written record of the checking process exist,"[6] observed Sam Rosenman. There was meticulous checking and cross-checking of information cited in this speech, fact checking made possible by a new U.S. Signal Corps car attached to the train for communication back and forth to Washington. FDR was careful about the content of the Chicago speech, which in essence laid out expansive domestic policy that he expected to follow the war. No one at Soldier Field would ever forget the speech. The ordinary capacity of the field was about 100,000 people, but no fewer than 125,000 were in attendance that night, "to say nothing," said Rosenman, "of the uncounted thousands who were outside the walls of field."[7] To Rosenman, the Chicago speech was the most dramatic example of the range and power of the president's speaking ability. The masses hung on every syllable. "Tonight I want to talk simply to you," said the president, "about the future of America—about this land of ours, this land of unlimited opportunity." Those who saw Roosevelt in Chicago had to be ticketed. The ticket shown here is one of them. (Author's collection.)

President Roosevelt and Prime Minister Churchill plan the Atlantic Charter, Roosevelt's fingers forming the "V for victory" symbol Churchill made famous by an apt coincidence. Roosevelt is caught in conversation with Churchill at their momentous conference on August 10, 1944. Directly behind them are Admiral Ernest J. King (left), commander in chief, U.S. Fleet, and General George C. Marshall, commander in chief, U.S. Armies. Beside King and Marshall is British General Sir John Dill (far right). (Official United States Navy Photograph. Author's collection.)

her life were made by the end of Eleanor's first year without Franklin. It was Fala, Roosevelt's beloved Scottie, who never really adjusted to his master's passing. "Once, in 1945, when General [Dwight D.] Eisenhower came to lay a wreath on Franklin's grave, the gates of the regular driveway were opened and his automobile approached the house accompanied by the wailing of the sirens of a police escort. When Fala heard the sirens, his legs straightened out, his ears pricked up and I knew that he expected to see his master coming down the drive as he had come so many times."[84] She also recounted that Fala, when they had moved into the cottage, always lay near the dining room door, where he could watch both entrances just as he had done when FDR was there. "Franklin would often decide suddenly to go somewhere," she continued, "and Fala had to watch both entrances in order to be ready to spring up and join the party on short notice." While the little Scottie accepted Eleanor after Franklin Roosevelt's death, Eleanor noted that she was only a temporary replacement until Fala's master returned. "Many dogs eventually forget. I felt that Fala never really forgot. Whenever he heard the sirens he became alert and felt again that he was an important being, as he had felt when he was traveling with Franklin."[85] Fala was laid to rest in the rose garden at Hyde Park next to his master, and as Eleanor concluded, "I hope he is no longer troubled with the need for any readjustments."

While the world spent months adjusting to the end of fighting after his death, Franklin Delano Roosevelt thus became Moses in the Promised Land, denied the glory of peace after carrying his people through the dark days of world war. He wanted to be the one—the leader of his people—to win the peace, and FDR knew, postwar, that there would be infinite needs among nations forging the bonds of peaceful existence. He had been a shrewd negotiator and advocate of postwar coexistence among the great powers. The political entanglements he experienced on the international stage were nothing more than a rough game for a toughened competitor. No one can be nominated, let alone be elected, to the U.S. presidency unless he is a master at the game. To a degree, the ability to change, compromise, and even shadow the truth a little, goes to the heart of FDR's political success negotiating peace for the world postwar. "Politics is, after all," he said, "only a technique to achieve government. The science of politics," on the other hand, "may properly be said to be the science of the adjustment of conflicting group interests."[86] Death denied FDR his goal of seeing a United Nations, but his spirit lived on, thanks not only to Eleanor Roosevelt's intimate involvement in its formative years as the United States' first representative to the organization, but the public's memory. Roosevelt's speeches appealed mostly to the human heart, as in them, observed Maxwell Meyersohn, he proclaimed old truths, truths which the voices of the prophets had cried down through the ages; truths which had been forgotten in an overwhelmingly material twentieth-century world.[87] The most direct reflection of the president's humanity rests with his innumerable speeches, because it was in them that he breathed life into his principles and goals.

> **Unless the peace that follows recognizes that the whole world is one neighborhood and does justice to the whole human race, the germs of another world war will remain as a constant threat to mankind.**
>
> *Address to the White House Correspondents' Association, Washington, D.C., March 15, 1941.*

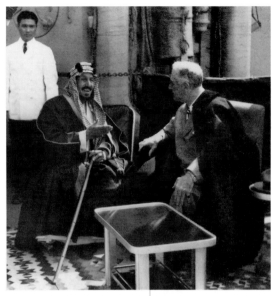

World War II eventually drew America into the Middle East. The president was most interested in meeting one ruler in the region, King Abdul-Aziz ibn Abdul-Rahman Al Saud of Saudi Arabia, generally called King Ibn Saud in the West. Here, Roosevelt meets with King Ibn Saud at Great Bitter Lake in Egypt on February 14, 1945. Roosevelt hopes that the king would help solve the looming question of the dispensation of Palestine were dashed, but their cordial February 1945 meeting led to the establishment of the two nations' informal security alliance. On March 1, Roosevelt went up to the Capitol to report on his meeting with King Ibn Saud. His health failing, Roosevelt's speech delivery was halting and full of ad-libs that were uncharacteristic of the president just four months before during his campaign—and victory—for a fourth term. Sam Rosenman observed that some of his extemporaneous remarks were wholly irrelevant, some even ridiculous. "The crushing effect of twelve years of the presidency was beginning to be more and more evident,"[8] wrote Rosenman. (FDR Presidential Library.)

The Little White House, Warm Springs. Ga.

K5141

Franklin Roosevelt built his Little White House, a pine-paneled six-room cottage, as his Warm Springs, Georgia, retreat in 1933. The president enjoyed the curative properties of the hot springs on the property, and it was here, on his forty-first visit on April 12, 1945, that he suffered a cerebral hemorrhage and died. (Author's collection.)

The funeral train arrived from Warm Springs, Georgia, on April 13, 1945. The funeral procession formed behind a caisson on which lay the flag-draped body of the commander-in-chief, Franklin Delano Roosevelt. Here, the caisson bearing the body of the president passes through the streets of Washington on its way to the East Room of the White House. Hundreds of thousands of Washington-area residents, some crying aloud, others weeping softly, stood dazed, hardly believing that FDR was dead. (John H. Kelly Jr., photographer. Author's collection.)

The structure of world peace cannot be the work of one man, or one party, or one nation. It must be a peace which rests on the cooperative effort of the whole world.

Address before Congress on the Yalta Conference, Washington, D.C., March 1, 1945.

After a brief and unpretentious funeral ceremony in the East Room on April 14, 1945, FDR's body was transported the following day to Hyde Park, and it is there (shown here) that the president was laid to rest in Springwood Rose Garden. Fala, the president's beloved Scottish terrier and constant companion, stood watch over his master's grave on many occasions. Even when the president lay dying at Warm Springs, five-year-old Fala had been sitting watchfully in the corner of the president's bedroom as FDR's doctors tried unsuccessfully to render him aid. Perhaps sensing the president's death, Fala suddenly leapt from his corner, "shook himself, crashed through a screen door and ran outside barking frantically till he reached the top of a nearby hill. There he stood vigil."[9] Mentioned in his speeches, and often in the press, Fala lived with Eleanor at Val-Kill until his death in 1952. The president's most loyal companion was buried next to his master, and is rightfully memorialized in the Franklin Delano Roosevelt Memorial in Washington, D.C. (Library of Congress. Author's Collection.)

President Harry S. Truman appointed former First Lady Eleanor Roosevelt as the first American representative to the United Nations (UN). Eleanor Roosevelt represented the United States at the UN from December 31, 1945, until December 31, 1952, when newly elected President Dwight Eisenhower asked for her resignation. As chairman of the Commission on Human Rights she was instrumental in the drafting of the UN Declaration of Human Rights, adopted by the UN General Assembly on December 10, 1948. Here, Eleanor Roosevelt confers outside the UN Central Hall at Westminster in London, England, in 1946. Though Eisenhower had replaced her, President John F. Kennedy reinstated Eleanor Roosevelt to her former UN post. Anna Eleanor Roosevelt died on November 7, 1962. "A shy, awkward child, starved for recognition and love, Eleanor Roosevelt grew into a woman with great sensitivity to the underprivileged of all creeds, races, and nations. Her constant work to improve their lot made her one of the most loved—and for some years one of the most reviled—women of her generation," states Eleanor's official White House biography. (FDR Presidential Library.)

The only limit to our realization of tomorrow will be our doubts of today. Let us move forward with strong and active faith.

Undelivered address prepared for Jefferson Day, to have been delivered on April 13, 1945.

Afterword *THE FDR LEGACY*

Most people thought of Franklin Roosevelt as an extroverted, gregarious man, when in reality, Eleanor theorized that he was basically a shy, reticent person. Son James Roosevelt disagreed with his mother until he gave it some thought, eventually drawing the same conclusion—his mother was right. What does this have to do with FDR's legacy, you ask? Everything. FDR had very few soul-searching conversations with any of his family members, including Eleanor, on matters other than public issues. "His was an innate kind of reticence that may have been developed by the fact that he had an older father and a very strong-willed mother, who constantly tried to exercise control over him in the early years," Eleanor once explained to James. "Consequently, he may have fallen into the habit of keeping his own counsel, and it became part of his nature not to talk to anyone of intimate matters." [88]

FDR, in large measure, kept no confidantes and was not a confidante to those around him. "He lived his own life exactly as he wanted it,"[89] Eleanor often told her children. But how did he get to be such an icon on America's political landscape? What makes FDR endure in the American consciousness over half a century since his death? In writing of his father shortly after his death, James Roosevelt told a story that offers one example of the humanity of the man who led the country through some of its most difficult times. "One of father's first orders when he moved into the White House was symbolic of the New Deal's humanity. He circulated word to

his staff, from the top secretaries to the telephone operators, that, if persons in distress telephoned to appeal for help of any sort, they were not to be shut off but that someone was to talk with them." The person on the other end of the line might be a farmer from Iowa who was about to have his mortgage foreclosed, or a homeowner in a big city about to lose his home, and if they felt desperate enough to telephone the White House, FDR wanted to render them assistance if help could be found. He was keenly aware of the suffering of the people he'd seen on the

campaign trail. In the end, FDR found ways to cut the red tape for American citizens who called him, and after his death, Eleanor Roosevelt received letters from strangers who told her how, in the darkest days of the Depression, they telephoned their president and received aid—and comfort. This, in short, was what the New Deal was about—it was government by humanity, observed James, not by slide rule or advertising agency. In the end, millions of Americans, as well as many people in other parts of the world, felt that Franklin Roosevelt was their personal friend. Those he'd never met or who'd never seen him felt a kinship with the American president.

Roosevelt maintained this unbreakable bond with multitudes of human beings that knew him only as a voice on the radio, perhaps a picture in the newspaper or a magazine, or a flash on a newsreel screen. But how did he become such a living, comforting presence in countless homes across America? After all, the United States had had popular presidents in the past, yet none achieved as strong a personal understanding with his followers as what developed between Franklin Roosevelt and the average American citizens who were attracted to his political and social philosophy—his way of doing business.

FDR was set apart from his predecessors by several factors, each of which impacts his enduring legacy as the longest-serving chief executive in American history. Prior to President Calvin Coolidge, presidents of the United States did not have the ready means of communicating with the public that was made possible by the radio. Roosevelt began using radio addresses as governor of New York to communicate issues to the public—and it was at that juncture he inaugurated his "fireside chats." Before Roosevelt's first term, presidents made their greatest impact on constituents only within range of voices, according to presidential scholars. "Even the most famous of former presidents were not particularly endowed with heart-warming, personable qualities that FDR came to personify," wrote Maxwell Meyersohn in 1950.

FDR had an impactful, powerful personality that Meyersohn noted had been brought out by cataclysmic events marking his entrance into and stewardship in the White House. Absolutely, by anyone's estimation, it was his use of the spoken word, especially on

THE TEST OF OUR PROGRESS IS NOT WHETHER WE ADD MORE TO THE ABUNDANCE OF THOSE WHO HAVE MUCH; IT IS WHETHER WE PROVIDE ENOUGH FOR THOSE WHO HAVE TOO LITTLE

the radio, that gave millions their sense of friendship and intimacy with him. Roosevelt knew, in short, how to express his most humane and democratic qualities. "It was this combination of moral purpose and pervasive skill that helped to gain him the public's confidence in his ability and integrity as a leader."[90] Roosevelt sensed an obligation—a devotion—to the American public, and his love of country reached far back in his own personal history. Historians have remarked often that FDR's inheritance and training had completely immersed him in American culture and tradition. He had, after all, ancestors who'd come over on the *Mayflower* and still others on both sides of his family who had been in America before 1776. He was

steeped in Americana and reveled in it. "Remember," he once told a gathering of the Daughters of the American Revolution, "remember always that all of us, and you and I especially, are descended from immigrants and revolutionists."[91] Roosevelt had an abiding sense of Americanism, noted Meyersohn, and American history, both of which to FDR were a functioning reality, not "the vague myth it is [today] for most children who are fed on it year after year from dry, unimaginative textbooks." No, FDR had, at the heart of it, a "penetrating and sympathetic knowledge of all kinds of Americans."[92] Some have observed this was remarkable for a man who, in his privileged beginnings, was tutored until the age of fourteen, attended preparatory school at Groton, and had a Harvard education. But as Roosevelt himself once remarked, a man's real education begins after his formal schooling ends; and Roosevelt's real education began in his late twenties when he entered local politics.

Franklin Roosevelt liked to be with people and he liked even more to talk to them, learning early the value of "give-and-take" in a community democracy. As president, FDR would share his views of this democracy with reporter and friend, Frank Kingdon, a conversation Kingdon said later was perhaps the most important he'd ever have with Roosevelt. "You and I know," said the president, "that democracy was a concept born in an agricultural society that had a much simpler organization than ours. Nobody was very rich and nobody was very poor when Jefferson and the rest first gave us a truly democratic state. There were no big cities and big corporations with crowded populations and hundreds of thousands of employees. Neighbor knew neighbor. Employers knew their workers and their families and took care of them when they were sick. It was all simple and easily handled, comparatively. Nowadays," he concluded, "we have a different kind of society. The Industrial Revolution and all that has flowed from it has changed the ways people live and their relationships to each other."[93] As Roosevelt saw it, his job was to make the essence of democracy, the part of it that is pure in any society, in all kinds of society, work in America. "I think it's my job to find out [how an idea born in an agricultural community can be applied in a highly industrialized one], and to do my best to make what changes have to be made without sacrificing the basic freedom of individuals, without making government itself too strong while making it strong enough to keep private concentrations of wealth and power from depriving people of their rights, or treating people as commodities in the marketplace."[94]

As FDR's political career flowered from New York onto the national scene, he traveled in all parts of the United States, wanting to know his fellow Americans—"my friends" as he would later call them. Roosevelt read accounts of people's problems, issues, needs, and hopes and even, on occasion, their far-flung dreams, and while he occasionally spoke directly to them, the president had good sources in just about all corners of the country. He connected with the public—the best evidence of this is the thousands of letters he received in the White House from those with whom he'd built a rapport across the heartland of America, largely through his oratory rather than direct, personal contact. He mingled

friendliness with his advisors' best research, creating a persona people could like—and vote for. By Eleanor's pointed account, her husband had no real confidantes nor did she feel she filled that role either. FDR was a man who, speechwriter and playwright Robert Sherwood concluded, guarded "a thickly forested interior."[95]

In 1938, on a swing through Maryland, Roosevelt said, "You cannot make men believe that a way of life is good when it spreads poverty, misery, disease, and death. Men cannot be everlastingly loyal unless they are free."[96] He believed that free men will always choose

wisely. At the dedication of his—the first—presidential library in 1941, FDR stated this article of his faith: "To bring together the records of the past and to house them in buildings where they will be prepared for the use of men and women in the future, a nation must believe in three things:

"It must believe in the past.

"It must believe in the future.

"It must, above all, believe in the capacity of its own people so to learn from the past that they can gain in judgment in creating their own future."

But the impactful side of his personality clearly cloaked his inner reticence for personal attention and protected his most private thoughts. The sea was FDR's greatest love, and he often retreated to it, away from the public that so adored him. The sea became the source to which he could turn when the burdens of the presidency became too great and his body and spirits needed lifting. The American public came to identify Roosevelt with this love of the sea. "I was with him on a number of his presidential cruises, both official and unofficial. In retrospect, I still marvel at how one almost could see his weariness disappear when father got the smell of saltwater in his nostrils and the feel of a rolling deck under him,"[97] remembered son James. The sea did more than restore Roosevelt's body; it brought out in him, in addition to a daring spirit, playfulness rarely associated with presidential dignity. He was

FDR the man, not FDR the president, when on the water. "Eleanor never shared his passion for the sea."[98]

By the third term, FDR's loneliness increased due to the deaths of his oldest friends, as well as his eighty-seven-year-old mother, Sara Delano Roosevelt, in September 1941. He tried to make new friends, and often reached back to the past to renew old relationships, searching always for the spark of friendship, but in the end kindling his most successful new relationships among exiled royalty and movie stars, including Katharine Hepburn. Hyde Park grew to mean more to him, and he often spoke of childhood memories with his staff and children.

So private was FDR that after he'd been buried at Hyde Park, Eleanor discovered an envelope in his safe addressed to James. James opened it and saw that it was a handwritten, four-page document of instructions for his funeral should he die in office. It was dated December 26, 1937—early in his second term when he was in good health. But the instructions were opened too late, as he'd never told Eleanor of them. She did, however, have a fairly good idea of what he wanted for a funeral. FDR wanted simplicity, a ceremony attended in the East Room only by the immediate family, the household, executive office staff who had been close to him, by the cabinet and their families and by other members of the administrative branch who had maintained a close relationship to the president. This was not fully observed, as those in attendance far outnumbered what he'd envisaged. And most of his children were in the military and out of the country. Only Eleanor, their daughter Anna R. Boettinger, and son Elliott were actually present from the immediate family as James, John, and Franklin Jr. were overseas at the time of his death. James tried, but missed the actual ceremonies. None of the grandchildren were there, as Eleanor wanted them to remember him as he'd been on his last inauguration day. But America would remember him always.

His second instruction, "that there be no lying in state anywhere," was followed. He had wanted his White House funeral followed by a simple service in the Capitol rotunda, but this was not done. The list of FDR's wishes detailed specifics down to his desire not to have his body embalmed or the casket enclosed in a vault in the ground. James learned all that reading the letter his father had never discussed with anyone openly. He speculated that his father likely felt following traditional liturgy was best: "Earth to earth, ashes to ashes, dust to dust, in sure and certain hope of the Resurrection."[99] FDR had also asked that his interment take place where the sundial stood in the rose garden, and that the casket

be carried to the garden by men from the estate including the Boreel property purchased by his grandfather, James Roosevelt, in 1868, and adjoining the land on which FDR was born, and the back farms and Val-Kill Cottage. Eight men from the armed services, as it turned out, bore his casket instead, but with interment as he'd requested.

James Roosevelt sums up his father's imprint on America best, his own grief tumbled with that of the country his father sculpted from depression and war. "I may as well ask myself how or when I will stop remembering Pa. Or when the people whom I meet wherever I go in this country and in other countries will stop approaching me and saying: 'I never met him, but I knew him. . . .' Or when strangers will stop saying: 'Let me tell you what your father meant to me. . . .'

"I could relate the details of how Pa drew his remarkable will," wrote James in *Affectionately FDR*, "of which he named me the family trustee, wording it rigidly to protect the principal of the estate for Mother during her lifetime, for he knew so well her impulsive, overgenerous instincts and did not want her to give everything away. I could write of how Mother, instead of lapsing into lonesome, idle widowhood, has become an even greater personality than she was at the time of Father's death. I could write of all the things that have happened to my sister, my brothers, and me. Some are good," he'd say, "some are bad, and many—perhaps both the good and the bad—can be traced to the way in which Pa raised us." But all of it would be anticlimactic, what James called "a wordy appendix" to his thoughts of his father. A fitting end to the FDR story—his legacy—comes from the words of Franklin Delano Roosevelt himself.

FDR was working on an address the day before he died, a speech that he was to have delivered by radio two nights later on the occasion of Jefferson Day dinners held throughout the country. "I think those who knew FDR best are agreed that he identified himself with [Thomas] Jefferson more than any other president," wrote Frank Kingdon. "Some may say that this was because Jefferson was founder of the Democratic Party, but I think this a superficial judgment. This identification came because Roosevelt felt that he was implementing in our society the principles to which Jefferson devoted himself in his generation."[100] FDR had once called Jefferson an "apostle of freedom." During his dedication of the Jefferson Memorial in 1943, Roosevelt said, "Generations which understand each other across the distances of history are the generations united by a common experience and a common cause. Jefferson, across a hundred and fifty years of time, is closer by much to living men than many of our leaders of the years between." In the April 12, 1945, draft of the Jefferson Day speech, he spoke not of partisan politics but of peace and patriotism. Roosevelt read a typed copy of what he had dictated for the Jefferson Day address, which was never fully finished, and was not, of course, ever delivered. "The last two paragraphs of this speech," wrote Judge Sam Rosenman, "should have been included in the prayers at his grave."[101] They would be the president's last words to the country—and to the world. He added the last sentence to the original draft in his own hand, perhaps his most fervent hope for all of us in the end. The last two paragraphs, truly his creed, read thusly:

Today, as we move against the terrible scourge of war—as we go forward toward the greatest contribution that any generation of human beings can make in this world—the contribution of lasting peace, I ask you to keep up your faith. I measure the sound, solid achievement that can be made at this time by the straight edge of your own confidence and your resolve. And to you, and to all Americans who dedicate themselves with us to the making of an abiding peace, I say:

The only limit to our realization of tomorrow will be our doubts of today. Let us move forward with strong and active faith.

Endnotes

1. Rosenman, p. 87.
2. Schlesinger, p. 1.
3. Ibid., p. 338.
4. Rosenman, p. 108.
5. Ibid., p. 164.
6. Ibid., p. 493.
7. Ibid., p. 496.
8. Ibid., p. 528.
9. Gunther, p. 371.
10. Roosevelt, Eleanor. *This I Remember*, p. 66.
11. Ibid., p. 71.
12. Ibid.
13. Roosevelt, Eleanor. *This I Remember*, Ibid. Louis Howe had been FDR's assistant at the Navy Department—and a close friend. When FDR was stricken with infantile paralysis, Howe put aside plans to take an oil company job to be by Roosevelt's side.
14. Simkins.
15. Rosenman, p. 3.
16. Ibid., p. 4.
17. Ibid.
18. Ibid., p. 5.
19. Rosenman, p. 8.
20. Rosenau, p. 265.
21. Rosenman, p. 11.
22. Mahl, Thomas E. and Roy Godson. *Desperate Deception: British Covert Operations in the United States, 1939–44* (Brassey's Intelligence & National Security Library). London: Brassey's, 1998. Commentary by Dr. Stephen J. Sniegoski, article for WTM Enterprises, January 11, 2000.
23. Rosenman, p. 549.
24. Gunther, p. 377–378.
25. Ibid., p. 378.
26. Rosenau, p. 1.
27. Roosevelt, Eleanor. *This I Remember*, p. 72.
28. Ibid.
29. Ibid., pp. 72–73.
30. Rosenau, p. 263.
31. Ibid.
32. Von Drehle, p. E17.

33. Roosevelt, Eleanor. *This I Remember*, p. 73.
34. Rosenman, p. 65–66.
35. Ibid.; p. 66.
36. Rosenau, pp. 263–264.
37. Ibid., p. 264.
38. Rosenman, p. 89.
39. Ibid., p. 90.
40. Ibid., p. 91.
41. Ibid., p. 88.
42. Rosenau, p. 265.
43. Roosevelt, Eleanor. *This I Remember*, p. 73.
44. Rosenau, p. 265.
45. Ibid.
46. Kingdon, p. 23.
47. Ibid., p. 26–27.
48. Ibid., p. 27.
49. Ibid., p. 64.
50. Ibid., p. 65.
51. Meyersohn, p. 10.
52. Rosenman, p. 95.
53. Roosevelt, Franklin D., p. xi.
54. Ibid.
55. Meyersohn, p. 12.
56. Kingdon, pp. 16–17.
57. Rosenman, p. 103.
58. Ibid., p. 107.
59. Ibid.
60. Ibid., p. 108.
61. Ibid., p. 144.
62. Ibid., p. 164.
63. Ibid., p. 166.
64. Kingdon, pp. 54–55; Rosenman, p. 243.
65. Rosenman, p. 261.
66. Kingdon, p. 233
67. Ibid., p. 44.
68. Ibid., pp. 57–58.
69. Ibid., p. 28.
70. Rosenman, p. 327.
71. Day, p. 386.
72. Rosenman, p. 474.
73. Roosevelt, Eleanor, *This I Remember,* p. 338.
74. Rosenman, p. 527.
75. Ibid., p. 537.

76. Rasmussen, p. 2D.
77. Roosevelt, Eleanor. *This I Remember*, p. 344.
78. Gunther, p. 371.
79. Rasmussen, p. 2D.
80. Roosevelt, Eleanor. *This I Remember*, p. 345.
81. Ibid.
82. Roosevelt, Eleanor. *On My Own*, p. 9.
83. Ibid.
84. Ibid., pp. 9–10.
85. Ibid., p. 10.
86. Meyersohn, p. 15.
87. Ibid., p. 18–19.
88. Roosevelt, James and Sidney Shalett, p. 236.
89. Ibid., p. 315.
90. Meyersohn, p. 4.
91. Ibid., p. 5.
92. Ibid., p. 7.
93. Kingdon, Frank, pp. 68–69.
94. Ibid., p. 69.
95. Olasky.
96. Kingdon, p. 72.
97. Roosevelt, James, and Sidney Shalett, p. 274.
98. Ibid.
99. Ibid., p. 367.
100. Kingdon, p. 115.
101. Rosenman, p. 551.

Bibliography

BOOKS

Brandeis, Erich. *Franklin D. Roosevelt, the Man*. New York: American Offset Corporation, 1936.

Brown, John Mason. *The Ordeal of a Playwright: Robert E. Sherwood and the Challenge of War*. New York: Harper & Row, 1968.

Bullitt, William C. *The Great Globe Itself*. New York: The Macmillan Sons, 1946.

Casey, Steven. *Cautious Crusade: Franklin D. Roosevelt, American Public Opinion, and the War Against Nazi Germany*. New York: Oxford University Press, 2001.

Churchill, Winston S. *The Gathering Storm*. Boston: Houghton Mifflin Company, 1948.

———. *Their Finest Hour*. Boston: Houghton Mifflin Company, 1949.

Day, Donald. *Franklin Roosevelt's Own Story*. New York: Little, Brown & Company, 1951.

Eddy, William A. *F.D.R. Meets Ibn Saud*. New York: American Friends of the Middle East, 1954.

Gunther, John. *Roosevelt in Retrospect*. New York: Harper & Brothers, 1950.

Halprin, Lawrence. *The Franklin Delano Roosevelt Memorial*. San Francisco: Chronicle Books, 1997.

Ickes, Harold L. *The Autobiography of a Curmudgeon*. New York: Reynal & Hitchcock, 1948.

Johnson, Gerald W. *Roosevelt: Dictator or Democrat*. New York: Harper & Brothers, 1941.

Josephson, Emanuel M. *The Strange Death of Franklin D. Roosevelt*. New York: Chedney Press, 1948.

Katz, Lee and Irving I. Friedman. *The Pictorial Life of Franklin Delano Roosevelt: Protector of World Freedom*. New York: The Virson Company, 1945.

Kingdon, Frank. *As FDR Said*. New York: Duell, Sloan & Pearce, 1950.

Mahl, Thomas E. and Roy Godson. *Desperate Deception: British Covert Operations in the United States, 1939–44* (Brassey's Intelligence & National Security Library). London: Brassey's, 1998.

McIntire, Ross T. *White House Physician*. New York: G. P. Putnam's Sons, 1946.

Meyersohn, Maxwell, ed. *The Wit and Wisdom of Roosevelt*. Boston: The Beacon Press, 1950.

Moley, Raymond. *After Seven Years*. New York: Harper & Brothers, 1939.

Moscow, Warren. *Politics in the Empire State*. New York: Alfred A. Knopf, 1948.

Nesbitt, Henrietta. *White House Diary*. New York: Doubleday & Company, 1948.

Perkins, Frances. *The Roosevelt I Knew*. New York: The Viking Press, 1946.

Rausch, Basil. *The History of the New Deal, 1933–1938*. New York: Creative Age Press, 1944.

Roosevelt, Eleanor. *It's Up to the Women*. New York: Frederick A. Stokes Company, 1933.

———. *On My Own*. New York: Harper & Brothers, 1958.

———. *This I Remember*. New York: Harper & Brothers, 1949.

———. *This Is My Story*. New York: Harper & Brothers, 1937.

Roosevelt, Elliott. *As He Saw It*. New York: Duell, Sloan & Pearce, 1946. Foreword by Eleanor Roosevelt.

———, ed. *F.D.R. His Personal Letters*. Early Years. New York: Duell, Sloan & Pearce, 1947.

———, ed. *F.D.R. His Personal Letters*. Volume II, 1905–1928. New York: Duell, Sloan & Pearce, 1948.

———, ed. *F.D.R. His Personal Letters, 1928–1945* (2 volumes). New York: Duell, Sloan & Pearce, 1950.

Roosevelt, Franklin D. *On Our Way*. New York: The John Day Company, 1934.

Roosevelt, James and Sidney Shalett. *Affectionately, F.D.R.: A Son's Story of a Lonely Man*. New York: Harcourt, Brace and Company, 1959.

Rosenau, James N., ed. *The Roosevelt Treasury*. New York: Doubleday, 1946.

Rosenman, Samuel I. *Working with Roosevelt*. New York: Harper & Brothers, 1952.

———, ed. *The Public Papers and Addresses of Franklin D. Roosevelt*. 13 Volumes. New York: Random House, 1938 (volumes covering 1928–1936); The Macmillan Company, 1941 (volumes for 1937–1940); Harper & Brothers, 1950 (volumes covering 1941–1945).

Schlesinger Jr., Arthur M. *The Coming of the New Deal*. Boston: Houghton Mifflin Company, 1959.

Sherwood, Robert E. *Roosevelt and Hopkins: An Intimate History*. New York: Harper & Brothers, 1948.

Stimson, Henry L. and McGeorge Bundy. *On Active Service in Peace and War*. New York: Harper & Brothers, 1948.

Tugwell, Rexford Guy. *The Stricken Land*. New York: Doubleday & Company, 1947.

Tully, Grace. *F.D.R. My Boss*. New York: Charles Scribner's Sons, 1949.

Welles, Sumner. *The Time for Decision*. New York: Harper & Brothers, 1944.

ARTICLES, PAMPHLETS, DISSERTATIONS, AND SPEECHES

Dionne, E. J., Jr., "Roosevelt, America's original man from hope," *The Washington Post*, May 1, 1997.

Driscoll, Edgar J. and William P. Coughlin, "Richard Gilbert, at 83; professor, World War II economics architect," *The Boston Globe*, October 8, 1985, p. 59, obituary.

Editorial, "A Look in the Mirror," *Brainstorm NW*, September 1998.

Griffin, G. Edward, "The Grand Deception: Part Two—A second look at the war on terrorism," Freedom Force International, 2002.

Krakow, David M., "FDR and the Jews: The Vision and Reality," *Nativ*, Volume 12, No. 4 & 5 (69–70), September 1999, Ariel Center of Policy Research.

Krock, Arthur, "President Roosevelt is dead; Truman to continue policies," *The New York Times*, April 13, 1945.

Morrow, Lance, "Spy Master-in-Chief: Roosevelt's secret war details how FDR ran his intelligence networks—officially and otherwise," *Inside Politics with CNN*, posted October 8, 2001.

Olasky, Marvin, "Franklin D. Roosevelt: How His New Deal Undermined Philanthropy, Charity and Society," Capitol Research Center, April 1999.

Pappas, Theodore, "All the Presidents' Ventriloquists," *The American Enterprise*, January/February 1998.

Raico, Ralph, "FDR: The Man, the Leader, the Legacy, Part 4," *Freedom Daily*, August 1998.

Rasmussen, Frederick N., "FDR's paramour had a Maryland pedigree," *The Baltimore Sun*, January 18, 2003, p. 2D.

Roosevelt, Franklin D., Undelivered Jefferson Day Speech, April 13, 1945.

Schroth, Raymond A., "Great Guy," *Columbia Journalism Review*, November/December 1997.

Simkins, Scott, "John Steinbeck's Populist Aesthetic," Dissertation, 1998, University of Southern Mississippi.

Starr, William W., "From FDR, some timely words," *The Houston Chronicle*, September 2, 2002.

Von Drehle, David, "In address, a second chance to transcend the sound bites," *The Washington Post*, January 20, 1997.

Ward, Darrell E., "Like father, like son, Jeffrey F. Moley, MD, professor of surgery, carries on the warm bedside manner he learned from his dad," *The Record*, Washington University in St. Louis, October 18, 2002.

Index

A

Acheson, Dean, 19
Adams, John Quincy, 23
Al Saud, Abdul-Aziz ibn Abdul-Rahman, *61*
Alabama Polytechnic Institute, 30-31
Albrizio, Conrad A., 22
American Committee for the Protection of Foreign
    Born (ACPFB), 38-39
Anti-New Deal, 29-30
Atlantic Charter, 60

B

Barkley, Alben W., *27*
Baruch, Bernard M., 4, 59
Beer, Samuel, 13
Berle, Adolf A., 4, 18
Boettinger, Anna R., 70
Bredahl, Lorence N., *44*
Brown, Walter, 14
Bruenn, Howard G., 56
Buck, Frank H., *27*
Bullitt, William C., 19, 32, 38-42

C

Central Intelligence Agency (CIA) (See Office of
    Strategic Services)
Children's Theater Units, 33
Churchill, Winston S., 10, 47-49, *55*, *60*
Civilian Conservation Corps (CCC), 10, 28, *30-32*,
    41
Cohan, George M., 7
Cohen, Benjamin, 19, 38
Commission on Human Rights, 65
Committee on Economic Security, 27
Coolidge, Calvin, 67
Corcoran, Tom, 15, 19, 33, 38
Cove Creek Dam, 35
Cummings, Homer S., 27

D

Daniels, Jonathan, 57
Daughters of the American Revolution (DAR), 68
Delano, Frederic, 24
Democrat National Committee, 11, 14, 50
Democratic National Convention, 4-5, 12, 17,
    31-32
Dill, John, *60*
Dingell, John D., 27
Doughton, Robert L., *27*
Dust Bowl, *19-20*, 23

E

Early, Stephen T., 57
Eisenhower, Dwight D., *55*, 60, 65
Espencilla, Joe, 56
Executive Orders, 27, 35, 45

F

Fala, *cover*, 5, 60, *64*
Farm relief, 11, 28
Farm Security Administration (FSA), 53
Fechner, Robert, 30
Federal Reserve System, 27-28
Federal Project Number One, 33
Federal Theater Project (FTP), *33*
Firebagh, Phyllis Fay, *58*
Fireside chats, 5-8, 15-*16*, 17, 21, 23, 28, 44, 49
Flynn, Edward J., 42
Frankfurter, Felix, 19, 42
Franklin Delano Roosevelt Memorial, *cover*, *1-9*,
    64, *67-69*, *71, 73*
Franklin Delano Roosevelt Presidential Library,
    39, 56, 59, 69-70

G

Gilbert, Richard, 4
Grand Coulee Dam, 23
Great Depression, 5, 10, 18, 20-21, 23, 26, 28,
    33, 47, 66

H

Hannegan, Robert E., 50
Hepburn, Katharine, 70
High, Stanley, 15, 33, 38
Hill, Samuel B., 27
Hitler, Adolf, 44, 53
Homestead Act, 19
Hoover, Herbert, 15
Hopkins, Harry L., 6-7, 19, 22, 24, 27, 42, 59
Howe, Louis, 4, 46
Hyde Park, 13, 17, 39, 44, 49, 52, 59-60, *64*, 70

I

Illinois National Guard, 41
Inaugurations, *13-14*, 15, 17-18, 21, 26-27, 39,
    44-45,
Isolationism, 38, 40-41

J

Jefferson, Thomas, 72
Jefferson Memorial, 72
Johnson, Hugh, 4, 14-15

K

Kai-Shek, Chiang, 47-48
Kennedy, John F., 65
Kennedy, Joseph P., 19
Kieran, James, 14
King, Ernest J., *60*
Kingdon, Frank, 8, 23-25, 44, 46-48, 68, 72

L

LeHand, Marguerite A., 4, 11, 31
Lend-Lease Bill, 48
Leonardo Da Vinci Art School, 22
Lewis, David J., 27
Lewis, John L., 48
Lincoln, Abraham,
Lincoln Memorial, 57
Lindley, Ernest K., 14
Little White House, 53, *62*

M

MacArthur, Douglas A., 41
MacLeish, Archibald, 5
Marshall, George C., *41, 60*
McCloy, John J., 42
McGoldrick, Joseph, 4
McIntire, Ross T., 50, 56-57
Mercer, Lucy (See Rutherfurd)
Michelson, Charles, 14-15
Moley, Raymond A., 4, 13-15, 18-19
Monnet, Jean, 42
Morgan, W. Forbes, 4
Morgenthau, Henry, 4
Morgenthau, Henry, Jr., 4, 27
Moses, Robert, 18
Muscle Shoals, 48, 51

N

National Industrial Recovery Act, 18, 30
National Youth Administration (NYA), 33
New Deal, 4-5, 7, 10, 12, 14, 16-19, 22-24, 26-35, 39, 66
Norris Dam, *34-35*

O

Office of Emergency Management (OEM), 53
Office of Strategic Services (OSS), 8
Office of War Information (OWI), 49, 53

P

Palestine, 61
Patton, George S., *55*
Pearl Harbor attack, 40, 45
Perkins, Frances, 27
Pershing, John J., 41
Polio, 23-25, 50-51
Prettyman, Arthur, 56
Public Works Administration (PWA), 18, 30

R

Reconstruction Finance Corporation (RFC), 18
Reynaud, Paul, 41
Richberg, Donald, 39
Robinson, Joseph T., *13*
Roosevelt, Anna (See Boettinger)
Roosevelt, Eleanor, *4-5,* 10-11, *13-14, 15,* 18, 21, 23, 25, *30,* 33, 47-48, 52, *56-61, 57,* 64, *65-66,* 69-72
Roosevelt, Elliott, 59, 70
Roosevelt, Franklin D., *cover, 1,* 4-9, *10-25, 12-17, 23,* 26-33, *27,* 35-37, *36-37,* 38-55, *40-41, 43-46, 55,* 56-65, *56-61,* 66-72, *70*
Roosevelt, Franklin D., Jr., *17,* 59, 71
Roosevelt, James, *17,* 59, 66, 70-72
Roosevelt, John, *17,* 59, 71
Roosevelt, Sara Delano, 70
Rosenman, Samuel I., 4-9, 12, 14-15, 17-20, 22, 28, 30-33, 38-40, 42, 44, 49-50, 52-53, 59, 61, 72
Ruppel, Louis, 14
Rutherfurd, Lucy Mercer, 56-57

S

Second World War, 40-42, 44-50, 52-55, 58, 60-61
Shangri-La (later Camp David), 55
Sherman, William Tecumseh, 30-31
Sherwood, Robert E., 6-8, 19-22, 42, 69
Shoumatoff, Elizabeth, 56
Social Security Administration, 29
Social Security Bill, 27
Stalin, Joseph, 47, 53
Steinbeck, John, 5
Stephenson, William S., 8
Stryker, Roy Emerson, 53

T

Teheran Conference, 49
Tennessee Valley Authority (TVA), 28, 34-35, 48, 51-53
Thompson, Malvina, 25
Thoreau, Henry David, 18
Tri-Borough Bridge, *18*
Truman, Harry S., 57, 59
Tugwell, Rexford G., 4, 18
Tully, Grace, 4, 6-7, 12, 23, 49, 57

U

United Nations (UN), 50, 61, 65
USS *Indianapolis* (CA-35), *43*
USS *New Mexico* (BB-40), *44*

V

Val-Kill Cottage, 59, 64, 71
Virginia, University of, 41

W

Walker, Frank C., 4, 56
Wagner, Robert F., *27*
Wallace, Henry A., *27*
Warm Springs, 13, 52-53, 56-58, 63-64
Watts, Williams, *54*
Welles, Sumner, 41, 44
Wheeler Dam, *50-51*
White House Correspondents' Association, 47, 49, 61
Willkie, Wendell, 24
Wilson, Woodrow, 38-40
Wilson Dam, 35, 51
Woodin, William, 19
Works Progress Administration, 22, 33

Y

Yalta Conference, 25, 52-53, 63

About the Author

A writer, former naval intelligence officer and wartime commentator, Amy Waters Yarsinske has published over two dozen books with a variety of presses and contributed to many others. Her most recent, *No One Left Behind: The LCDR Michael Scott Speicher Story*, was released in July 2002 by Penguin Putnam/Dutton in hardcover, and in May 2003 in softcover with an update of the Speicher case. Yarsinske's telling of the Speicher story has received international acclaim by reviewers—and readers alike. In the book, Yarsinske delves deeply into the story of how Scott Speicher was lost over the western Iraqi desert on the first night of the 1991 Persian Gulf War. "Of course," wrote one reviewer, "no one had looked for him, and no one would—not for years. Now, it seems, he may have been alive all along—and a prisoner of Saddam Hussein. 'Spike' Speicher had done more than fall from the skies over Iraq. He had fallen victim to indifference and incompetence, then to lies and intrigue for more than a decade." The audio book edition of *No One Left Behind* won *Publishers Weekly*'s Listen Up Award 2002 for nonfiction, and is a finalist for *ForeWord* Magazine's Nonfiction Book of the Year. Prior to the book's publication, Yarsinske's six-part feature series with Lon Wagner on Scott Speicher—"Dead or Alive?"—ran on the front page of *The Virginian-Pilot* from December 30, 2001, through January 4, 2002, and garnered Yarsinske and Wagner a Pulitzer Prize nomination and a Virginia Press Association award for feature writing. Ms. Yarsinske has investigated the Speicher case since 1993.

Born in Norfolk, Virginia, on December 21, 1963, Ms. Yarsinske received her Bachelor of Arts degrees in economics and English from Randolph-Macon Woman's College in Lynchburg, Virginia, and a Master of Planning degree from the University of Virginia School of Architecture, where she was a DuPont Fellow. She is a member of the

Authors Guild, Investigator Reporters and Editors (IRE) organization, and an inductee into the Virginia Center for the Book's distinguished Virginia Authors Room. Yarsinske is represented by Robert G. "Bob" Diforio of D4EO Allen O'Shea Literary Partners LLC. She is married to a former active duty naval flight officer—now a reservist—and Gulf War veteran. They have three children.

About the Contemporary Photography

Carol M. Highsmith, a world-renowned photographer, provided the cover image and additional photography on pages 1-8, 66-69, 71 and 73. Highsmith took all of these images at the FDR Memorial in Washington, D.C. During the course of her career, Highsmith has become the preeminent photographer of the nation's capital, capturing the city's stunning architecture and treasure landmarks for posterity. The author gratefully acknowledges her contribution to this book.